DAVID DILLARD-WRIGHT, PhD

A MINDFUL MORNING

*Start each day with a
clear mind and open heart*

Adamsmedia

AVON, MASSACHUSETTS

Published by
Adams Media, a division of F+W Media, Inc.
57 Littlefield Street, Avon, MA 02322. U.S.A.
www.adamsmedia.com

ISBN 10: 1-4405-9636-0
ISBN 13: 978-1-4405-9636-0
eISBN 10: 1-4405-9637-9
eISBN 13: 978-1-4405-9637-7

Printed in China.

10 9 8 7 6 5 4 3 2 1

Library of Congress Cataloging-in-Publication
Data
Dillard-Wright, David, author.
A mindful morning / David Dillard-Wright, PhD.
Avon, Massachusetts: Adams Media, [2016]
Includes bibliographical references.
LCCN 2016007749 (print) | LCCN 2016014520
(ebook) | ISBN 9781440596360 (pb) | ISBN
1440596360 (pb) | ISBN 9781440596377
(ebook) | ISBN 1440596379 (ebook)
LCSH: Meditation.
LCC BL627.D553 2016 (print) | LCC BL627
(ebook) | DDC 204/.35--dc23
LC record available at
http://lccn.loc.gov/2016007749

The information in this book should not be used
for diagnosing or treating any health problem.

Not all diet and exercise plans suit everyone.
You should always consult a trained medical professional before starting a diet, taking
any form of medication, or embarking on any
fitness or weight-training program. The author
and publisher disclaim any liability arising directly or indirectly from the use of this book.

Many of the designations used by manufactur-
ers and sellers to distinguish their products are
claimed as trademarks. Where those designations appear in this book and F+W Media, Inc.
was aware of a trademark claim, the designations
have been printed with initial capital letters.

Cover design by Frank Rivera.
Cover images © 2004 Visual Language, iStock-
photo.com/flas100, iStockphoto.com/beakraus,
iStockphoto.com/CSA-Printstock, iStockpho-
to.com/katyau, iStockphoto.com/blueringmedia.
Interior images © 2004 Visual Language,
Nongnuch Leelaphasuk/123RF, David
Methven Schrader/123RF, iStockphoto.com/
macrovector, iStockphoto.com/Alioshin,
iStockphoto.com/tomograf, iStockphoto.com/
flas100, iStockphoto.com/123dartist,
iStockphoto.com/elyaka,
iStockphoto.com/nicoolay, iStockphoto.com/
daboost, iStockphoto.com/Zenina,
iStockphoto.com/aleksandarvelasevic,
iStockphoto.com/duncan1890,
iStockphoto.com/Slanapotam,
iStockphoto.com/Craig McCausland,
iStockphoto.com/katyau.

*This book is available at quantity
discounts for bulk purchases.
For information, please call 1-800-289-0963.*

Per ardua

•

Contents

Introduction

In devotional Hinduism, the hours before dawn are thought to be among the most auspicious for meditation, as the veil between the divine and human worlds is the thinnest during these hours. The morning rituals serve as purification for the day to come, to set the mind on the right track. Taking a few moments in the morning to collect your thoughts and check in with your emotions can do wonders for your ability to manage and dismiss stress throughout the remainder of the day. The modern rituals of drinking coffee and reading the news also prepare the mind to face the challenges ahead, and these, too, can be met with mindfulness. Mindfulness, an intentional and steady embrace of the present moment, comes from within.

Few of us claim to be *morning people*, but perhaps we haven't given ourselves permission to savor the early hours, to appreciate the light of a new sun. The reflections in *A Mindful Morning* come from a variety of world philosophies and religions, and they will help you start each day intentionally. These moments of centering will help take the sting out of the morning commute and pressing schedule by easing you calmly into your day. Over the course of this book, you will develop strong inner reserves that help you remain at peace despite the trials of our frantic society, so you can move throughout the day consciously and purposefully as your best and most authentic self.

You may think that you do not have time for mindfulness or meditation, but just think about how much time you spend reading random bits of news and Internet ephemera. Think about how much time you spend tweeting or going on Facebook, or playing *Minecraft* or *Candy Crush*. Think about the time that you spend sorting through mostly nonvital e-mail. Think about the stuff that you have to do: compiling reports for work, taking care of the kids, paying bills, buying groceries, doing the laundry; the list goes on and on. You deserve a break of a few minutes, several times a day, to collect yourself and put your mind in a calmer state. You deserve a break from the constant stream of noise and information.

I wrote this book thinking that you, dear reader, have lots of competing priorities—that you do not, in fact, live in a hermitage on top of a mountain. I imagine you sneaking a few minutes here and there to center yourself. I imagine you setting down your cell phone and finding that comfortable chair or reading nook. I see you lighting a stick of incense for a brief time of sacred silence. I see you at your desk or cubicle grabbing a minute or two to take some deep breaths and engage in thoughtful reading. Know that, wherever you are, you stand at the center of the struggle of the ages learning how to live a peaceful life in the midst of the hectic world. May you find a welcome respite in these pages.

But I'm Not a
Morning Person . . .

Most of us think of morning as time to be endured or rushed through quickly. We try to be as highly caffeinated as possible, to drop off the kids, to make the commute, and maybe catch the weather and the news along the way. Very few among us would confess to being a *morning person*, which sounds like a sort of mythical beast, the unicorn of the twenty-first century. It's not very cool to be a morning person. Confess to loving to wake up in the morning around the coffee pot at work and prepare yourself for scowls and murmurs. We think of morning people as Pollyanna types who whistle "Zip-A-Dee-Doo-Dah" on the way down the front walk, past the picket fence and the rose bushes, which, of course, they stop to smell. Get real. Who has time for that? Crack open a can of Red Bull and get in the f*#king car!

And so the day begins, with an aggressive cast of mind, with a heavy foot on the accelerator. When the morning hours are full of stress and anxiety, the rest of the day follows in that pattern. No wonder we seek to escape through entertainment. No wonder we medicate through junk food, prescriptions, and booze. But I'm not here to preach or moralize. Rather, let's seek to understand the true nature of the problem and move beyond it.

We should probably start with sleep. According to A. Roger Ekirch's fascinating history *At Day's Close: Night in Times Past*, staying up late at night didn't become very practical until the advent of electric lighting. All of those candles and oil lamps were expensive and apt to catch fire, so people generally went to bed much earlier. People in preindustrial societies largely slept in two sessions with a break in between. It was quite common to rise in the night and spend some time in quiet reflection, perhaps reading a book, saying prayers, or engaging in more (*ahem!*) carnal activity. Going to bed and rising were timed with the sun, which meant more sleep in winter and less sleep in summer. The *watches of the night*, those nocturnal waking hours, were like bonus free time. But night held more terrors like the fear of burglary or fire, which were both more common before streetlights. With electricity, we came untethered from the sun and could arrange our time accordingly. For many of us, this is simply convenient and has little downside. For others, like medical professionals and factory workers on the night shift, working at night means permanent disruption of sleep, with many mental and physical health side effects.

These days, we tend to sleep in one big block, rather than two smaller ones, but the size of the block gets smaller as the years go by.

With our electronic devices and overabundance of entertainment, we sleep less. The Centers for Disease Control and Prevention (CDC) classifies insufficient sleep as a public health problem, with the lack of sleep interfering with work, hobbies, and basic safety on a massive scale. In 2005–2007, thirty percent of adults reported getting six hours or less sleep per night, a level of sleep deficit associated with higher levels of chronic disease and even increased mortality. In daily life, not getting enough sleep reduces concentration and memory, which means that nearly every task becomes more difficult. So perhaps the exercises in this book should begin with trying to get more sleep. Completing these little meditations probably requires going to bed a little bit earlier and rising a little bit earlier. We're not talking hours here: You can start with five to ten minutes, probably less time than you spend in the shower each morning.

We shouldn't idealize the morning, but we also shouldn't discount it. It is never easy to awake from sleep, and yet those early hours do have an impact on the day. We measure our lives in years, in days, in hours, in minutes, and to dismiss part of the day is to look a gift horse in the mouth. So maybe you won't immediately become a *morning person*, whatever that means, but you might learn to get a little more out of the early hours. Not for reasons of productivity per se, but to just enjoy life a little more, to find more satisfaction in the daily grind.

If you think of the mornings as times for yourself, rather than for the proverbial *man*, you might be inclined to get out of bed more nimbly.

Mindfulness: More Than Meditation

The trouble with the word *meditation* is that it implies, for many people, an activity that is conducted separately from the rest of everyday life. Meditation implies an idyllic setting, perhaps a monastic vocation, and usually a religious frame of mind. There is certainly nothing wrong with tradition, religion, or monasticism, and people who come from ancient traditions certainly have a lot of guidance to offer to lay practitioners. The trouble with viewing meditation as separate from daily life is that it implies a dualism between spiritual life and everyday life. It builds a wall of separation between the sacred and the profane. The goal of meditation should be to look upon every act as sacred, to see every moment as holy, and to view each person, place, and thing as a manifestation of the divine.

One of my own teachers, Shree Maa of Kamakhya, Assam, is a lifelong devotee of the great Bengali saint Sri Ramakrishna. She tells a story that helps us remember the sacred in the midst of everyday life. When Shree Maa was a little girl, she had a large share of the household responsibilities like cooking and cleaning. She recalls in *Shree Maa: The Life of a Saint*:

One day I was sweeping the floor, and when I had finished cleaning the rooms, I threw the broom into the corner where it was kept. Immediately I heard the voice of Sri Ramakrishna calling to me from within. 'Hey there! That broom is your very good friend. Why do you treat it with such disrespect? If it weren't for his loving service, how would you clean your house?' Quickly I went over to the corner, picked up the broom, and said, 'Namaskar, I bow to your divine essence.' Gently I placed it back in its proper place, and from that time on, I tried to regard each and every thing as a manifestation of divine grace.

Shree Maa points us to our hasty, thoughtless attitudes in order to pay attention to the harshness in our actions. If we conduct ourselves more reverently, the whole tenor of life begins to change. In place of the default annoyance that characterizes our daily interactions, a sort of inner glow begins to emerge, one where I regard each new situation as the way to say *namaskar* (a spiritual greeting) to the universe. The divine interfaces with me through the medium of everyday things and situations. This frame of mind can be held only through great difficulty, but it is a much more satisfying way to live than regarding every encounter as a personal affront.

Taking Refuge in the Present Moment

One of the foremost names that people associate with contemporary mindfulness practice is the Vietnamese Buddhist monk and peace activist, Thích Nhất Hạnh. He has written dozens of books, but the basic point behind his practice is to be fully engaged in the present moment. We begin with conscious breathing, but ultimately each and every small action becomes part of mindfulness practice. In *Peace Is Every Step: The Path of Mindfulness in Everyday Life*, Thích Nhất Hạnh tells the story of a group of children meditating on tangerines that he brought for them. Each child is invited to think of the blossoms of the tree where the tangerine grew, the fruit slowly ripening in the sun, the person picking the tangerine, and finally the fruit right there in front of them. The children peel the fruit slowly, seeing the fine mist erupt from the peel and the white pith beneath. They take each bite with intention, tasting the sweetness and the sourness of the juice in their mouths. Children probably need less prompting to live in this way than most adults, since they have not had the time to grow jaded and world-weary. Through mindfulness, we can come to see the world again with the eyes of a child, to look upon each moment as something new and bright, not to dull the senses, but to awaken them. The mind, too, is a sense, for it helps us see the vast networks of interconnection that make this moment possible.

One of the key voices of mindfulness in the Christian tradition is Brother Lawrence, who recorded his experiences in a book called *The Practice of the Presence of God*. As a monk, Brother Lawrence was not a typical spiritual adept. If monks had a batting average, his would be rather terrible. On his knees before the sacrament at mass, he didn't feel much of anything. He dreaded going on retreat because the experience was just dull and dry for him. His spirituality came alive for him in the kitchen where he cooked for the other monks. There, at his work, he would hold secret conversations with God, and the work itself became his form of prayer. His holiness grew palpable, and people would come for miles around just to watch him work in the kitchen. *Ora et labora*, pray and work in Latin, goes the Benedictine motto, and perhaps the two are interchangeable when completed with the right attitude.

The words *God, gods, divine,* and the like might intimidate those who come from secular backgrounds. If that is the case, think about it like this: Things just go better when you put your full capacities behind your efforts. You can think of these religious words as underlining or highlighting the beauty and mystery all around us. If these words get in the way for you, think of them as calls to pay attention, to focus. The parents at a Little League game yell, "Keep your eye on the ball, Johnny!" Walking around half-distracted is like taking your eye off the ball. You still get things done, yes, but not as well as you might have. And not only that, distraction also saps the enjoyment from life. It's just hard to enjoy something that only has part of your attention. If you decide to watch a television program, great! Just put your full attention into what you are doing. If you are walking the dog, put your full attention into walking the dog. It's just that simple, and yet that very simple-in-theory lesson can be very difficult in practice. We are so used to having a divided mind that it can be hard to return to full presence.

Hitting the Pause Button on Life

Sometimes it can be difficult to think of daily life as a kind of prayer or meditation. Bad things happen, people do annoying things, and we all get bent out of shape from time to time. Most of us have jobs that are unrelenting, and we have families to support. We can't all get away for a week's vacation, or even a weekend. But what if you could actually slow down time? Then you could turn five minutes into an hour, an hour into five hours, and so forth. That would be magical, right? You could still get everything done and be a sane person at the same time. I am here to tell you that you have this magical power at your disposal, and it is called meditation or mindfulness.

You are probably already rolling your eyes, but give me a second to explain. First of all, I am talking about lived time, or what is called in philosophy *phenomenal time*, time as experienced. You may not be able to put the entire world on pause, but you can pause your own little part of it. When you close your eyes and shut out distraction, a funny thing happens. The seconds lengthen, you can feel your own heartbeat, and the synapses between the moments grow longer, almost as though you were living in time-lapse photography. If you don't believe me, try setting a timer for one hour. Sit there quietly, not doing anything else, just paying attention. If you have never done this before, that hour will seem like days.

In my house, we have a clock in the kitchen right above the back window. The clock is powered by a single AA battery and has actual hands. Most of the time, the clock is ignored. Our kitchen is the focus of much hubbub throughout the day, as meals are prepared and laundry is folded for our family of five. The dog comes and goes, and the kids wage lightsaber battles. We look at the clock in the morning to see just how late we are running; the rest of the time it just hangs there. But when I get up in the middle of the night or early in the morning, and I sit down to meditate—not in the kitchen but in the living room, at least thirty feet away and past walls and doorways separating the rooms—I can hear that clock ticking. When I start doing my *pranayama*, it actually seems quite loud, so it can be difficult not to hear it. I can really grasp the length of a second, its duration, of which I am usually completely unconscious. I enter into a different state of mind, one in which I become the observer.

I know, I know. You can't always sit down and close your eyes. You have to drive your car. People at work can be nosy. Yada yada. But you can do the same thing with eyes open. In just a few moments, you can enter that meditative frame of mind in which you become aware of your surroundings, aware of your breath, and aware of the passage of time. You can deliberately expand those moments so that they seem longer to you: In *your* reality, time will be passing more slowly, even if no one else knows about it. A few minutes of meditation are qualitatively different from a few minutes of watching *Downton Abbey* or clicking through a random website. This same mindfulness can then be brought into whatever you happen to be doing throughout your day. When you are first beginning, you will need peace and quiet, but you can gradually learn to be mindful even in very hectic environments. Yes, it would be nice to have a vacation on the French Riviera, but it is good to have a few minutes just to be human, whatever the circumstances.

Stress Relief Through Contemplation

It can be useful to think about the mind in terms of carrying capacity. The human brain can handle many different inputs and process a great amount of information, but its capacity, at some point, will be overtaxed. At this point, the limbic system kicks in, sending out the hormones that produce the familiar fight-or-flight response. On the fight side, anger and frustration arise, while, on the flight side, perhaps fear, depression, or anxiety will manifest themselves. In a state of stress, the body prepares its defenses: the pulse quickens, the stomach knots, breathing becomes shallow. These defenses, when activated over long periods of time, produce a variety of mental and physical ailments that are quite common in consumer societies. Our minds are complex and resilient, but not infinitely so. Eventually, breakdowns will occur.

Mindfulness practice can be a good way to reduce stress so that it does not become chronic and debilitating. The stressed mind races thinking of consequences that have not yet occurred. The stressed mind asks, "What if I can't pay my bills?" or "What if I don't get this project done in time?" The mind that has come back to itself through mindfulness practice asks, "What is here right in front of me?", "What is it that I need to pay attention to at this moment?" Mindfulness practice can bring the mind to present realities rather than suppositions about the future. Once the hypotheticals, the feelings of impending doom, have been tamed, more *bandwidth* will be left to deal with the problems that might actually be present. Putting your complete self into the present moment allows for more graceful and complete responses to challenges that arise, so that you are not permanently stuck in crisis mode. Over time, and with a lot of practice, mindfulness training leads to improved health and performance, but most of all, it increases your level of enjoyment in life.

How to Use This Book

I've prepared this book with the thought that you will read one exercise/reflection per day. Each day begins with a quote from an expert or a scripture, followed by a thought for the day and something concrete that you can do in your daily practice. Try to go to bed a little earlier each night and rise a little earlier, but no more than thirty minutes earlier than usual. I have intentionally not put a specific time frame for most of the exercises. On days when you are feeling rushed, you can take five minutes. If you have some more time, take twenty minutes to an hour. You can make your way from the front of the book to the back, select a page at random, or choose a meditation based on the topic. You can keep the book in your home meditation area, on a bedside table, or in your desk at work. The important thing is to establish a routine so that when you find yourself in your chosen space, an automatic feeling of relaxation will come over you. This begins to happen after you get into the practice of meditating at the same place and time.

Interruptions will occur frequently, and conditions will not always be ideal. You may not be able to control every aspect of your surroundings, but you can choose how to react to the stimuli that come into your life. Perhaps you live with a lot of city noises or bright lights. This does not have to be a bad thing: You can make what might be considered distracting into a part of your practice. As you strengthen your mindfulness muscles, you will tolerate less-than-ideal conditions better. You will not so much *tune out* distractions that create an idea of separation and rigidity—as you will allow whatever strong sights and sounds to pass through you. It's as though you become lighter and more transparent. You don't have to put a lot of effort into resisting distractions because you have transcended the thinking, grasping mind. You will still be *there*, present in the situation, but you will cease plotting and planning. As your routine agendas drop away, your ability to sit still and listen will increase.

You may experience rapid progress at first, where you feel intense feelings of harmony and bliss. This may go away after a few weeks, and mindfulness will seem routine, even boring. Resist the temptation to go back to a distracted, fragmented way of living. You may be doing the most important work when it feels like nothing is happening. When the restlessness gets to be too much, do something active like taking a walk or making yourself a cup of tea. But make these activities, too, part of your practice.

Of course, you will have to attend to all of your daily responsibilities. Try not to assume any new duties, but keep the commitments that you have at work and at home. The exercises in this book will teach you a new way of seeing, a new way of being, that is not dependent upon accruing more status symbols or résumé items. You will find yourself caring less what other people think, although it will always be good to be kind to them. As you get unstuck from your own issues, you will be in a better position to be able to help others.

Whether you consider yourself a *morning person* or not, this book will help you approach the day with a sense of ease, possibility, and expectation. You will be able to let go of that sense of impending doom and go about your life with a sense of lightness and grace.

Exercise Your Mind

Possessing a creative mind . . . is something like having a border collie for a pet: It needs to work, or else it will cause you an outrageous amount of trouble. Give your mind a job to do, or else it will find a job to do, and you might not like the job it invents (eating the couch, digging a hole through the living room floor, biting the mailman, etc.).

Elizabeth Gilbert, Author

It only takes a few minutes to realize that your mind doesn't have an on/off switch. As Elizabeth Gilbert says, it's more like a large and energetic dog. Our minds give us the most fabulous experiences with their rambunctious frolicking, but they can also be quite destructive.

To give your mind something to do, put it to work noticing beauty and joy in the world. Right now ask it to put aside the depressing headlines from the day's news, the hurtful comment that a colleague made at work, the list of items you need to buy at the grocery store. Ask it instead to think of ten beautiful things it has encountered in the last twenty-four hours, and ask it to go on noticing beauty throughout the day to come.

Responding to Failure

*The way in which man [sic] approaches his failure
determines what he will become.*

Karl Jaspers, Philosopher

Silicon Valley has of late embraced entrepreneurial failure as a path to improvement and eventual success, but we all know that failure can be painful and discouraging. Every person alive has defining failures in his or her past. Not all of these failures will be surmounted: Some will permanently define the personality of the person who has suffered them. We need not even see these failures as obstacles to be overcome: Perhaps they are just part of our psychic makeup like mental wallpaper. We can identify many types of failure, some that prove to be transformative, and others that block our growth for years. Mindfulness practice can help to develop clarity about failure.

Give yourself permission to reflect for a few minutes on one defining failure in your life. Is this failure simply something to be discarded, or is it something to be overcome through more strenuous effort? Make a resolution to meet your failure not through regret or self-blame, but through concrete action taken in the present. Brainstorm a few steps you can take to leave your past in the past and make a new start.

Hear the Silence Around You

Sages send the spirit to the storehouses of awareness and return to the beginning of myriad things. They look at the formless, listen to the soundless. In the midst of profound darkness they alone see light; in the midst of silent vastness, they alone have illumination.

Huai-nan Tzu

As twenty-first-century humans, we can be pretty uncomfortable with unoccupied time, with empty spaces, with lingering silences. We like to have every single second filled with information, with words, with entertainment, and yes, with meaning. We have forgotten to pay attention to the silences, to the spaces between the words, to the unintelligible. And yet, what would music be like without any rests? How could the river flow to the sea without the low places? In meditation, we train ourselves to sit silently, to listen to the apparent nothingness of background noise.

Eventually, if conditions are just right, we can hear and feel the blood rushing in our ears, the high *eee* sound of thought, the *lub-dub* of the heart muscle, the inhalation and exhalation of breath. What appeared to be silence actually becomes the subtle music of the surroundings, the beating heart of this moment, and the dance of the cosmos. If we can resist running away from the initial awkwardness of silence and stillness, a new way of being emerges, one that is more patient, more attentive, and more joyous. This is the light that emerges from darkness, the speech that comes from silence. Set a timer for five to ten minutes and sit as quietly as you can. See if you notice the rhythms of your own body and the little sounds that often go unnoticed. See if you can listen without commenting.

Embrace Change

Accepting change correctly brings us into harmony with reality . . . which is what happiness is really about. Being in touch with, in harmony with, reality is being in harmony with God—the ultimate reality. The aim of all spiritual practice is to enable us to experience this fullness and dynamism . . . concretely, whether in washing the dishes or chanting the Psalms.

The Monks of New Skete

One of the major troubles in the practice of meditation is to want to hold onto pleasant interior experiences, to want bliss all the time. Inevitably, the *high* moments fade, even though we crave them like junkies seeking a fix. Observing the world, we notice that everything is in flux, every state passes, things change. We must learn to let cherished things, people, and experiences come and go like the wind. We must open our hearts so widely that we do not hinder change from happening, so that we do not try to freeze our relationships or circumstances in place.

Quickly make a list of three changes that have happened in your life. These may be upsetting, traumatic changes, or they may be load-lifting, hopeful changes. Hold these changes before your mind's eye and cultivate an inner attitude of loving and embracing change. Picture your powerful, loving heart taking the edges off life's transitions so that they become more smooth and natural. Cherish the most loving course of action, and see yourself gracefully accepting change into your life.

Find Calm in the Storm

Our emotions and thoughts are like the weather. They are sometimes pleasant, sometimes unpleasant, always changing. We can do little to control them directly, and are wise not to try. . . . And after the occasional, inevitable storm has passed, we only need to quietly watch as the clouds dissipate on their own without any help from us.

Steve Hagen, Roshi of the Dharma Field Zen Center

Most of us would not try to wrestle a live alligator, and we would not try to play chicken in moving traffic. We would never get into a rowboat and steer it toward a hurricane. And yet we readily plunge into the storms of negative thoughts when they arise, thinking in vain that we can manage them and make them conform to our wills. You may think the analogy is not apt because, after all, thoughts occur inside our own heads. Our thoughts, you might think, are the very contents of ourselves. And yet they come and go as they like, and we are not very adept at controlling them. The trick of meditation, if there is a trick, is to regard thoughts as something external like the weather or like a passing crowd. No matter what happens, avoid identifying with the thoughts. Regard them as *out there*, not *in here*. You might pretend the thoughts are like the weather or like a birthday party full of spoiled, screaming three-year-olds! You can watch the kids, but you don't need to get in the ball pit yourself.

Our emotions and thoughts
are like the weather. They are
sometimes pleasant, sometimes
unpleasant, always changing.

We can do little to control them
directly, and are wise not to try. . . .

And after the occasional,
inevitable storm has passed,
we only need to quietly watch
as the clouds dissipate
on their own
without any help from us.

—STEVE HAGEN, ROSHI, DHARMA
FIELD ZEN CENTER

As long as you think you can control your thoughts, you will have no rest. As soon as you just let them do their thing, you will begin to have peace. Set a timer for five to ten minutes and see what arises for you this morning as you sit silently. Whether the thoughts are angry or passionate, trivial or profound, just let them come and go. If you make a mistake and find yourself trying to wrestle them, gently move yourself back into the mode of listening and observation.

Encourage Yourself to See the Divine Mother

The fair lovely word "mother" is so sweet and so kind in itself that it cannot truly be said of anyone or to anyone except of him and to him who is the true mother of life and of all things. To the property of motherhood belong nature, love, wisdom, and knowledge, and this is God.

Julian of Norwich, Christian Mystic

Images of the divine matter, for they shape whether we view the world as a nourishing, welcoming place or a competitive, harsh reality. Envisioning God as mother opens our minds to the possibility of an all-encompassing, caring presence, which, in turn, opens our minds and hearts to the possibility of caring for human and nonhuman others. A self-fulfilling prophecy happens when we view God as either a nurturing mother or a harsh taskmaster: As we see God, so we see the world, so we see ourselves.

Spend a few minutes at the opening of the day quietly meditating on the idea of God as mother. Experience her presence in the curl of leaves on a tree, in the sound of falling rain, in the rising and falling of breath. Remember that she has her guises, her play: She reveals herself when she chooses, not according to our timetables. Keep in mind throughout this day that she may reveal herself unexpectedly, turning some chance encounter into a brush with divinity.

Radiate Love and Peace

The entire chain is one. Down to the last link, everything is linked with everything else; so divine essence is below as well as above, in heaven and on earth. There is nothing else.

The Essential Kabbalah, *Trans. Daniel C. Matt*

A stone thrown into a pond will send ripples out to the very edge, until every last bit of its kinetic energy has been dissipated throughout the surface of the water. The disruption is transmitted across the face of the water until it is spent and released. In the same way, each and every action touches everything else: We are all part of one massive system that encompasses all things. Some choose to label this interconnectivity as nature, others as God, and others still as energy. We may view this reality poetically, scientifically, religiously, or perhaps some of all three. No matter how you look at it, this moment connects in so many ways to other moments, to other beings that may be half a world away.

This interconnection need not be frightening or paralyzing: We might be inspired by it instead. Since all of our thoughts and actions radiate outward in time and space, we should do our best to make our impacts as positive as possible for those around us. Starting from the heart center, cultivate feelings of peace and love for all beings. Picture this loving energy radiating outward to touch the whole universe. Try to hold this attitude for a few quiet minutes before beginning your day.

Move Beyond *If Only*

*Either you look at the universe as a very poor creation out of which
no one can make anything or you look at your own life and your own
part in the universe as infinitely rich, full of inexhaustible interest,
opening out into infinite further possibilities for study and contemplation
and interest and praise.*

Thomas Merton, Trappist Monk

Have you ever said to yourself, "If I only had more time . . . ," or "If I only had more money . . . ," or "If I only lived in a more interesting city . . . ." These negative forms of self-talk really amount to justifications for failing to live a fully engaged life, for failing to work with the materials at hand. We can all live vibrant, awake, fulfilled lives if only we look down into the deepest reserves of our souls and bring into the light the treasures that are stored within. There is nothing sentimental or sweet about this task: It takes great fortitude and courage to live with creativity and integrity.

Take a few minutes to examine your own *if only* statements. Try to ferret out the half-truths that you tell yourself to keep from having to fully deal with life. Imagine what it would be like to stop saying *if only* and take some small action today. Meditation and action are two sides of the same coin: Action implements what you have heard in silence. Meditation eliminates busywork and useless action as the focus sharpens.

Dealing with Resentment and Anger

Creating an enemy imparts a sense of control—we feel superior, we feel right, we believe we are doing something about the problem. . . . Yet if we lash out with hatred and violence . . . we generate more fear, reactivity and suffering. Freeing ourselves from this trance of fear and alienation becomes possible only as we respond to our vulnerability with a wise heart.

Tara Brach, Buddhist Teacher, Psychologist

Think of a frequently recurring resentment or anger, something that arises for you on a regular basis. At first glance, it may seem that the other person causes your anger, and yet, on a deeper level only *you* can control the emotions that arise from your reaction to the situation. Notice the unpleasantness of anger and resentment, as well as the ultimate futility of such feelings. (After all, they largely do not affect the person they are directed toward.) Then inquire into the origin of these feelings. What do you get out of nursing old injuries? Why do you fan the flames of anger?

For a minute or two, see if you can isolate the circumstances in which your anger and resentment arise. Resolve to insert a few deep breaths between the stimulus that occasions the anger and the reactive, emotion-laden thought that follows. You will begin to feel more relaxed as you plan to deal with the situations in your life more productively.

True Renunciation

*For one to whom the world has ceased to exist, neither is there
causing of injury, nor forgiveness, neither pride nor dejection,
neither wonder nor perturbation of spirit.*

Ashtavakra Gita

Renunciation of anxiety is a positive step in opening your heart to living mindfully. Thinking of gain, we leave our place of rest and go chasing after many things. Fearing loss, we flee from unseen, even nonexistent enemies. Always chasing after this and that, always running from this and that, we have no contentment, no peace, or tranquility. Giving up the bright and shiny things, giving up dark and heavy fear, resting calm and contented in the heart center—this is the only way to find liberation. Renunciation must cut two ways, not trusting in pleasure, yes, but also never really believing that the fearful object is worthy of fear.

Practice gathering your attention into the heart center by observing your breath. Each time you feel either aversion or desire, simply bring your mind back to your breath. Open an empty space in the heart, and, if you find yourself feeling restless, take note of the feeling without doing anything about it. Return to the calm center of yourself now, in the quiet, and come back to it throughout the day.

What Are Your Real Needs?

Hope is not an individual fantasy or a recourse to a romanticized and unrealistic view of the world. On the contrary, it is a subversive force that enables those who care about humanity, dignity, and ecological sustainability to act in concrete ways to defend and advance them.

Henry A. Giroux, Scholar, Cultural Critic

Society constrains minds and hearts by dictating what is thought to be practical or impractical, common sense or insane. Mindfulness practice can make us alert to the manipulation machine in which we live every day. Mindfulness makes us awake to what really matters rather than the product currently being sold—whether the product is a new shampoo or another war. Mindfulness makes us respond to reality rather than fantasy, and hence it inoculates us against a wide variety of lies.

In these quiet morning moments, pay attention to the rising and falling of your breath, to the little sounds of your home, to the feeling of the morning air on your skin. See how little you really need: some food, water, and shelter. Realize that every being needs the same things. Resolve to have no enemies, to feel superior to no other creature, and to have no desires other than the fulfillment of true needs.

Be Grateful
for Spiritual Teachers

The merits of pilgrimages, fasts and hundreds of thousands of techniques
of austere self-discipline are found in the dust of the feet of the Holy.

Sri Guru Granth Sahib

We often become entangled in knots of our own making. Having become entangled in this way, we try to remove these knots ourselves, making them even worse. To untangle a knot, it is most useful to have good lighting and clear vision, to see exactly how the situation has arisen and how to best get out of it. For that reason, we seek the feet of holy people who can show the way out of the entanglements of life. These people, who have dedicated their lives to holiness and the service of others, have the true knowledge that brings release.

Take a few minutes to think back about the holy people who have crossed your path over the years. Take a minute to inwardly give thanks to them and seek their blessings. If you are fortunate enough to have one of these holy ones in your life at present, make a plan to visit your teacher or send a small gift. Ask your chosen divinity, or the universe, to give you the chance to be an inspiration to others so that you can one day return the favor.

Unite the Outside and Inside

There are three kinds of devotees: superior, mediocre, and inferior. The inferior devotee says, "God is out there." According to him God is different from His creation. The mediocre devotee says: "God is the Antaryāmi, the Inner Guide. God dwells in everyone's heart." The mediocre devotee sees God in the heart. But the superior devotee sees that God alone has become everything. . . .

Sri Ramakrishna, Hindu Saint

When thinking of ultimate reality, we often confuse our own thoughts with the reality itself. In order to capture that reality as best as possible, we must expand our minds as much as possible to encompass the entire universe. This can only be done by holding the most open frame of mind, to think that the mind and the body, the surrounding room, and the Earth and the atmosphere are all part of the unfolding of the divine nature. If we think in this way, nothing contains and nothing is contained, but God is everything.

As you sit and breathe deeply with your eyes closed, note that you can picture the world around you in your mind's eye. See your body become translucent, with only the most subtle boundary between your body and the world *outside*. Notice the interplay between the world as it appears to the senses and your mental representations of it: The inner and outer senses reinforce one another. Let your respiration tie together the *inside* and the *outside*.

Silence As Teacher

He cannot be spoken of, but he can be spoken to;
he cannot be seen, but he can be listened to.

Walter Kaufmann, Philosopher

Mindfulness exercises our *listening muscles*, our *paying attention muscles*. Mindfulness can be practiced while doing anything: paddling a kayak, teaching a class, walking down the street, or eating ice cream. It will be difficult to practice mindfulness while doing these other activities, however, without a solid foundation in silent listening. By setting time aside for sacred silence, we also make these other activities sacred. By forming the inner disposition of attentiveness, we can be attentive to external things too.

Take a few minutes, perhaps twenty or thirty, to sit in silent contemplation. Listen to the outer environment and listen to the inner landscape as well. Simply pay attention to whatever arises for you. You don't need to worry about whether or not you are doing the practice properly. Simply let silence be your teacher and guide. The only important thing is a desire to be present to the practice, to lean into the desire to make contact with reality in an unmediated manner.

Contemplation and Action

When we think of wars in our times, our minds turn to Iraq and Afghanistan.
But the bigger war is the war against the planet. This war has its roots in
an economy that fails to respect ecological and ethical limits—limits to
inequality, limits to injustice, limits to greed and to economic concentration.

Vandana Shiva, Scholar, Activist

In reality, there is no division between spirituality, ethics, and politics. You cannot be a good person without advocating for marginalized people, for the Earth, and for nonhuman animals. You cannot have peace within unless you make a serious effort to care for these others. You cannot have peace in your heart if your commitments do not align with your beliefs. We all must cultivate peace as an inner attitude, but we must also express that peace in concrete actions that transform society.

Think for a few minutes about what most bothers you about our world. Is it domestic violence? Religious strife? Cruelty to animals? Resolve to do something each day to act in accordance with your beliefs. You could do something simple like write an article or a letter. You could join an organization devoted to your cause, or you could volunteer for an organization that inspires you. Your concrete action will propel your spiritual life forward.

Overcoming Victim Consciousness

The way to bring an end to violence is to remove people's sense of injustice instead of urging them to engage in a struggle to achieve justice. Working justice is possible in all situations, whereas ideal justice is not.

Maulana Wahiduddin Khan, Islamic Spiritual Scholar, Activist

Violence begins with the predilection for nursing injury, rehashing a series of perceived wrongs committed in the past. This is just as true for interpersonal violence as it is for violence between nations. These forms of violence begin within the psychic space of imagining oneself to be victimized or martyred in some way. This is not to say that real wrongs do not occur in the world: We just have a choice about how to respond to them. We can choose the path of anger and aggression or the path of forgiveness and peace. Choosing the path of peace takes a great deal of effort in the internal sphere, as well as constructive action in the world.

Take a few minutes to consider your own mental space. Examine the times in which you have recited the wrongs done to you by another person. Note how quickly suffering follows upon the assumption of victim consciousness. Now examine a time in which you were able to act more constructively. See if you can tell the difference between the two responses.

Balance the Bitter and Sweet

When We give mankind a taste of Our blessing, they rejoice therein: but if they encounter tribulation because of their own actions—they fall into despair.

Qur'an 30 (Sūrah ar-Rūm):36

Life has twin aspects that cannot be separated: The bitter and the sweet must be taken together and accepted as one and the same reality in order to have any peace in life. The pomegranate fruit is surrounded with a thick and bitter rind. Without this rind, the delicate seeds inside could not survive the elements. So it is in our own lives: The difficulties that we curse so bitterly often cause our protection. Without them, we could not learn and grow. These difficulties in the school of life give us all of the lessons that we need to survive and thrive. How well we learn these lessons depends on our graciousness and our acceptance of circumstance.

Set a timer for two minutes and make a list of every possible complaint that comes to mind. Then, for ten minutes, write down the possible good that could come out of each negative circumstance. Try to balance your consciousness so that you accept everything on your list, even if you can't bring yourself to be happy about the difficulties you face.

Ignite Your Curiosity

For me, Gaia is a religious as well as a scientific concept, and in both spheres it is manageable. . . . God and Gaia, theology and science, even physics and biology are not separate but a single way of thought.

James Lovelock, Scientist, Originator of Gaia Hypothesis

A sense of wonder and curiosity unite the differing disciplines of human inquiry, all beginning with that simple question of *Why?* All of the great minds in human history have been restless seekers, unsatisfied with the status quo, wanting to push the boundaries of human knowledge and experience. Of course, in reality, there are no *great minds*, only communities of like-minded investigators. Yes, there is competition in the art world just as there is competition in the sciences, but even this fighting spirit advances the overall aims of the discipline, which is to say, the collective.

Reinvigoration of our spiritual and creative lives begins with two simple questions. First, *What do I want to know?* and second, *What am I willing to do about it?* Take a few minutes to think about each of these questions. If you like, record your responses in a journal entry. Then make a concrete plan of action based on this exercise. In order to increase your mindfulness in the world, you must first awaken your innate curiosity.

Try Chakra Yoga

It's as if we're living on the front lawn of our own home. We've been locked out of ourselves for so long that we forget there is a house to live in. . . . We've forgotten what a house is for. We've forgotten that there even is a house. We've forgotten that there is shelter inside of our own hearts.

Krishna Das, Bhakti Musician

Much meditation instruction begins by focusing on the *ajna* chakra, located just between the eyes. The trouble with beginning at this point is that most of us have been conditioned to identify with the brain or the mind as the self. We visualize the thoughts swirling there, between the eyes, and come to think of those thoughts as the self. It often works better to start at the *muladhara*, at the base of the spine, or at the *anahata*, in the heart center, picturing the chakras aligning as we sit upright. The inner darkness can pull the mind away from the *content* of consciousness to simple awareness.

As you breathe rhythmically and deeply, picture your inhalation filling the base of the spine with energy. As you breathe out, picture a white light moving up your spine and out the top of your head. After a few rounds of this deep breathing, pick either the *muladhara* or the *anahata* as a focal point. Allow your awareness to rest in this space, and picture your body growing translucent and luminous. Feel the weight of gravity rooting you to the Earth, and picture the axis of your spine going directly up into the sky. Continue building the intensity of the practice until you feel a great white light flowing through your body.

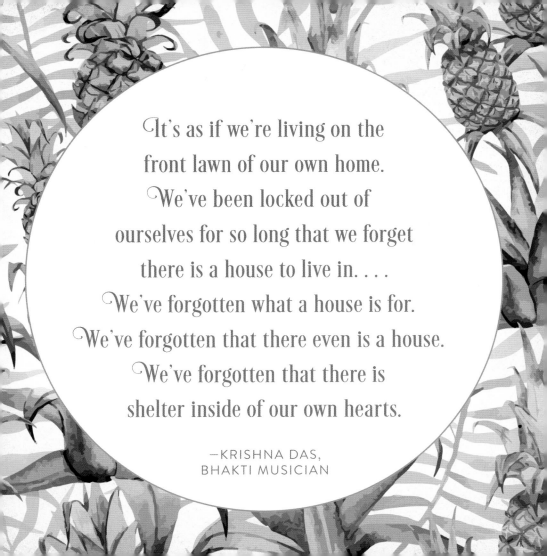

It's as if we're living on the front lawn of our own home. We've been locked out of ourselves for so long that we forget there is a house to live in. . . . We've forgotten what a house is for. We've forgotten that there even is a house. We've forgotten that there is shelter inside of our own hearts.

—KRISHNA DAS,
BHAKTI MUSICIAN

Equal Vision

*An enlightened person—by perceiving God in all—looks at a learned person,
an outcast, even a cow, an elephant, or a dog with an equal eye.*

The Bhagavad Gita 5.18

Much of our suffering in life arises from conditioning built into our personalities by societal expectations. If we look down on someone of lower standing, we may have lost a person who might have been a good friend or supporter. If we look down on animals and the natural world, we lose a great source of inspiration and delight. Or, on the contrary, if we have an overly low opinion of ourselves, we will be driven into despair and inaction. We must try to unlearn some of the bad lessons of the past in order to achieve a vision of equanimity, in which all beings deserve respect.

At the beginning of this day, resolve to say *namaste* (the God in me honors the God in you), to each person, animal, and thing you encounter. You do not have to say this out loud—just say this in your mind's eye. You may feel a little silly at first saying *namaste* to a teacup, but go ahead and try it anyway. Feel a greater sense of affection and warmth rise within your chest. Notice a certain gentleness suffusing your actions.

Respect Your Emotional Awareness

The ability to objectify feelings, so they are placed outside the political realm, is another reason people have not cared. Submission to authority requires such objectification—indeed, rewards it. Not only do people learn that feelings do not matter, but even the awareness of feelings is lost within the objectifying mind-set.

Carol J. Adams, Feminist, Animal Rights Activist

We should be on guard whenever we are warned of being too sentimental or too sensitive to the plight of others, whether they are near or far away, human or nonhuman. Claims to *objectivity* often mask certain callousness to the fate of others. Our emotions can sometimes be misleading, but they can also be good clues for how to act ethically in the world. Mindfulness practice can teach us how to sort the unhelpful emotions, which are often self-centered and melodramatic, from the helpful ones, which are other-directed and caring. We have to be careful, though, because some of the *self-centered* emotions are good as well: They can help us to detect when someone is trying to take advantage of our caring natures.

This morning, before the day has begun, pay attention to your emotional state. Are you feeling grateful, resentful, jealous, bored, stressed, or doubtful? See if you can use the most precise adjective possible. Sit with that emotion for a while, as though it were a welcome guest at your table. Note that you are separate from your emotions, and they can be helpful signposts along the journey of life. You need not either willfully suppress emotion or go along with it uncritically: Look at the information the emotions give you and then pause for reflection. Insert a pause between action and reaction.

Cherish Our Shared Destiny

Calm is the thought, calm the word and deed of him who, rightly knowing, is wholly freed, perfectly peaceful and equipoised.

Dhammapada 96

Once we begin to understand that we belong to other people and they belong to us, that the *inside* and the *outside* of the mind are the same thing, that the whole Earth and everything in it are caught up together in a common destiny, the great tumult of worry begins to subside. If you do not think of yourself as separate from the rest of nature, you no longer need to defend yourself from external threats. You no longer need to promote yourself as somehow being above and better than the rest of humanity. The defenses fall away as you realize that you are a part of the great drama of nature, and that you are not the doer. If you can hold onto this vision, you will have peace of mind and heart. As soon as you let go of it, anxiousness returns.

Gather yourself together by concentrating on your breath, which should be kept long and deep, with the exhalation equal to the inhalation. If you know techniques of breath control (*pranayama*), use them for a few minutes. Then choose a word like *calm* or *peace* and try to cultivate that state. Picture calm and peace enveloping not only you but the world around you as well.

Inbox, Outbox

Ambition is the humour most contrary to seclusion.
Glory and tranquility cannot dwell in the same lodgings.

Michel de Montaigne, Philosopher

Pity the miserable person who seeks to *make a mark on the world*. The world cares nothing about our plans for it: The crowd will gladly ignore our brightest and best contributions. Rewards and recognition will never substitute for the simple satisfaction of a job well done. We should resolve each day to go and do our best at whatever vocation or avocation awaits. The rewards will come and go like the tides, but there is always work to be done. Those with a spiritual cast of mind should think of prayer and meditation as manual labor, work that needs to be done.

As you sit for meditation this morning, think of your thoughts as having an *inbox* and an *outbox*. Do not actively encourage your thought process: Simply allow the thoughts to come as they will. The vast majority of thoughts will be inconsequential: Put them in the *outbox* and let them go. Occasionally a good thought will arise. Maybe you need to send a friend a *Get Well Soon* card. Put that in the *inbox*, meaning that you will return to it later. Do this for as much time as you have, perhaps ten to twenty minutes. Make sure to stay very light and easy with the thoughts, and do not inquire into them beyond this simple, mechanistic sorting process. As you get more adept, try to lengthen the silence that comes between the thoughts.

Venture Into Uncomfortable Places

So as long as our experiences come and go and we are investing in them our own values, thoughts, and emotions, we'll never find out if there is any truth in them, for truth is what remains when there are no experiences left.

Bernadette Roberts, Christian Mystic

Techniques of meditation and the thought processes that go along with them, such as *Am I pronouncing this Sanskrit word right? Did I sit long enough? Don't I really deserve a breakthrough by now?* etc., can be an unconscious defense against God or the Buddha, nature or silence, or whatever reality the practitioner is seeking to reach. Rarely do we just plunge ourselves headlong into a direct and unmediated being—present with the moment. If we do plunge headlong into this unmediated state, we usually expect immediate payback in the form of blissful experience. The idea that we might be bored or unsatisfied is very scary, even for experienced meditators.

When this sort of noise arises as you sit this morning, simply turn your attention away from it toward the silence, or toward whatever uncomfortable boredom awaits you. We usually need to visit the uncomfortable places in the surrounding stillness because it is there that we are trying to hide something. The cure is the medicine that can most be found in letting the light into these hidden, unexplored spots.

Defusing Resentment

When our energy is spent on imaginary fights with those who have wronged us, we are not present in our own day-to-day life. We have poisoned our own well.

Julia Cameron, Author

We spend much of our mental energy rehearsing for conversations that have not yet happened and may never happen. We also mentally replay key scenes from the previous days, weeks, and years, running different scenarios, asking, "What if I had said this . . ." We imagine that these exercises optimize our own advantage, but they actually sap the vitality out of life, making it hard to connect with reality. We really need to forgive others for past wrongs and accept our lives the way they are, but this is easier said than done.

Mindfulness practice brings to the work of forgiveness a sort of early intervention. By practicing mindfulness, we notice the obtrusive thoughts the moment they arise. Perhaps some of these thoughts will arise for you this morning as you read these lines. Simply say to the angry, resentful voice, "I acknowledge you, and you make some valid points, but I do not have time for you now." Then return your awareness to the present moment. With repeated practice, you will one day find that you no longer harbor the destructive thought pattern.

Reunion with the Present

The song that I came to sing remains unsung to this day.
I have spent my days in stringing and unstringing my instrument.
The time has not come true, the words have not been rightly set;
only there is the agony of wishing in my heart.

Rabindranath Tagore, Poet, Nobel Laureate

At the heart of mindfulness practice runs a deep longing to be free from a divided mind that does not live in the present—it always flees into the past or fantasizes about the future. It is strange that we should be so alienated from our lives, so distanced from the people and things right around us. The reunion of the practitioner with his or her own life can be framed as the longing of a lover for the beloved. Only deep devotion, and even passion, can make the moment of reunion happen.

Most of us have certain filters or preset attitudes of heart and mind with which we view the world. There is the hard-boiled skeptic, the naïve optimist, the practical realist. These interpretive frames actually preselect the aspects of reality that fit into that predetermined mold. If you had to describe your own personality in a few words, what would it be? Find some ways this morning to let go of your filters, and make every effort to perceive things the way they are.

Taming Your Inner Dialogue

The unjust word, unable to realize itself by creation,
realizes itself by destruction. It must either slay or be slain.

Eliphas Levi, Occultist

We think of the words that run through our heads as idle, inconsequential chatter. But words always retain something of incantation, of magic. Words affect our dispositions, sketch out actions, form affections. It would be ideal to have interior silence, but this takes a great deal of discipline and years of practice. In the meantime, taking all of this type of chatter with a grain of salt will be a good start. Then place a sort of mental seal over the thought forms, depriving them of their power. Eventually, the thoughts become less bristly, more luminous, and more benevolent.

This morning, in order to escape from the tug of the inner dialogue, make your senses your friends. Go outside for a few minutes and listen to the sounds of birdsong. Feel the breeze on your face. Notice the rustle of each blade of grass. Allow the senses to pull you out of your mind and into your body. Notice that the senses, often maligned, can be great aids to mindfulness.

Let Go of Predictions

How do we overcome fear? By giving up all practices in that direction.

H.W.L. "Papaji" Poonja, Advaita Vedanta Guru

To become mindful, to become awake, we must separate reality from our projections about reality. That can be quite difficult when we live inside our own projections. We can build for ourselves a grim reality, a dark world full of threats, but how many of them are real? We should seek to pare down our mental inventory to what we actually know; we should not read into every event some sinister plot. Rather than saying, "So-and-so must not like me very much," we could say, "So-and-so must be having a bad day." This depersonalizes the behavior and provides a more minimalist interpretation. We also have to look at our media diets and see how much negativity we absorb from sensationalist press accounts.

This morning, as you ease into your day, cultivate in your heart an attitude of openness and gratitude. Take note of any grim mental predictions that arise in your mind. This could be something like *I bet traffic is going to be terrible today* or *I'll never be able to finish all of the work that I have to do.* Let go of all such predictions and encounter the day as it is. Try listening to some music instead of the news.

Expand Your Vision

*You may have heard the notes of Man, but have not heard those of Earth;
you may have heard the notes of Earth, but have not heard those of Heaven.*

Zhuangzi, Philosopher

The task of mindfulness practice is the expansion of vision, making our connection with the world whole and complete. We aim to live in the more expansive Self rather than in a limited Self, realizing our connection to all things, animate and inanimate, creating a bond of kinship with the universe. We must escape from the fatalism that says, "I have seen all there is to be seen," and move rather into a stance of humility, which says, "I have as yet only scratched the surface of what is to be seen."

Today, as you encounter the first rays of morning light, picture yourself moving into infinite possibility. Know that your mind and senses are limited, and that you must, therefore, use them to their full potential. As you sit in meditation, or go quietly about your day, picture your six senses (sight, hearing, smell, touch, taste, and mind) growing ever more sensitive and expansive. Make it your job to notice the smallest details. Never let the smallest scrap of beauty, like a weed growing out of a sidewalk, go unnoticed.

Belonging to Others

That aspirant for liberation who, when engaged in activities in the world looks upon himself as a wave in the ocean that is Brahman, when just sitting thinks of himself as a gem strung on the thread that is Brahman (like pearls on a string), when experiencing sense objects through the sense organs sees all objects as Brahman (or Atman) alone and when sleeping considers himself as immersed in the ocean of bliss that is Brahman and spends his days in this manner is the one who is established in the indwelling self that is none other than Brahman.

Adi Shankara, Founder of Advaita Vedanta

Error and suffering arise when we think that we exist independently from others, that we can separate ourselves from the unfolding of existence, our support and origin. Liberation begins when we see that we are all enmeshed in something greater than ourselves, which may be called the universe or God or Shiva-Shakti. The egoistic person thinks to increase his or her power by withdrawing from the whole, but this only produces a kind of mania and a sudden or eventual downfall.

This morning, as you rise to greet the sun and sky, think of yourself as belonging to the universe and the universe to you. The trees, the grass, and the sky are your body and your mind: Your thoughts reach out to the swirling galaxies. The physical world that your eyes can see represents a tiny portion of reality, and all of that unseen energy makes your life possible. Billions of years of silent yearning made your life possible, and you are a moment in a great journey that will continue billions of years after you have left this body.

Disarm Negative Emotions

*Consider the "negativity flags" that keep coming up in your life.
There may be feelings of worry that need to be undone, or recurring
outbursts of anger . . . or feelings of self-pity and not being good
enough in some way. With active surrender, we will begin to see that
all the areas of negative energy are linked to the energy of fear,
vanity, or desire (greed).*

George Alexiou, Author

In order to move beyond negative emotions, we must understand that we get something out of them. They act as a kind of buffer or armor between our egos and the world, providing a feeling of security. It is easier to take a perverse feeling of comfort in being a victim, in being right, than it is to accept responsibility for our actions and thoughts. If I feel angry, I get the *payoff* of absolving myself of any culpability. But we pay a high cost for this dubious protection in the form of a reduced capacity to connect with other people and experience joy. To break out of this trap, the negative emotions must first be recognized and then released. This takes a lot of practice and continual effort.

Look at your interior landscape. What are the negative states that arise for you most often? What is the psychic *payoff* that you get from embracing such negative states? This morning, resolve to be more deliberate about the choice of thoughts and emotions you allow into your life. Notice that your thoughts and emotions are choices, are behaviors, and that you can take control of them, albeit with great effort and presence of mind.

Break Out of Your Routine

The call of the universe is like the pull of the sun on the sunflower, which causes the blossoms to open up and face the sun continuously as it crosses the sky. . . . It is the call to come up higher, to take charge of your life, to release your imprisoned splendor.

Eric Butterworth, Unity Minister, Author

The paradox of living as a human being is that we crave stability and comfort and yet strive to grow and change. When the stability impulse overpowers the growth impulse, we experience spiritual and creative starvation. Mental and emotional dullness become the order of the day. We need not be successful in our endeavors (in any measurable sense) in order to escape this dullness, but we do need to try to engage with life and make a difference. We have to move outside of routine and push the boundaries of our past experience.

Much of our dissatisfaction with life arises from ingrained habit. As your mindfulness assignment this morning, try doing something outside of your ordinary routine. Go on a new route for your morning walk, get coffee at a different shop, or wear a funky outfit. Savor the experience and note every detail. See if you can expand this *new and different* experience into other areas of your life.

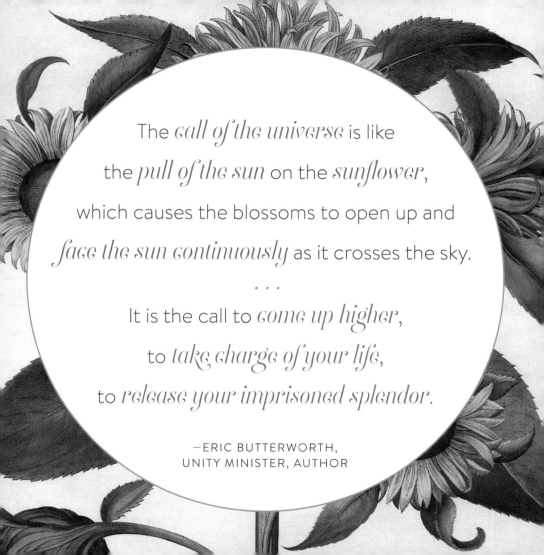

The *call of the universe* is like
the *pull of the sun* on the *sunflower*,
which causes the blossoms to open up and
face the sun continuously as it crosses the sky.

. . .

It is the call to *come up higher*,
to *take charge of your life*,
to *release your imprisoned splendor*.

—ERIC BUTTERWORTH,
UNITY MINISTER, AUTHOR

You Are Part of the Whole

This whole world is interwoven in Me; It is I that am the Ishvara that resides in causal bodies. . . . I am the Sun, I am the Moon, I am the Stars; I am beast, birds . . . and I am the Thief, I am the cruel hunter; I am the virtuous high-souled persons and I am the female, male, and hermaphrodite.

The Devi Gita

Those of us who were raised and educated in Western thought believe reflexively that we exist as separate, isolated individuals. It takes a great deal of study and meditation to see the myriad of forms of interconnection that make such an atomic conception of the person impossible. As we grow ethically, intellectually, and spiritually, we see ourselves as members of one another, part of one vast network that encompasses all living and nonliving things. Mindfulness practice helps us see the strands of this web that reaches outside the self. We come to experience a curious inversion in which the universe becomes ourselves.

As you practice this morning, note how the language of your inner dialogue has its origins outside of *you*. Notice how the air that you breathe originates beyond the confines of yourself. Note how the food digested in your body comes from outside of *you*. Continue in this process until you are aware that you can call nothing uniquely your own, that you belong to the whole.

Don't Worry about Technique

True meditation is neither concentration nor relaxation. We use concentration and relaxation to approach meditation, but in essence meditation happens by itself. You could say that concentration and relaxation are the means by which we approach the Infinite and Eternal, and that meditation is the result of the Infinite ever so briefly opening Its gates for our personal awareness.

Kosta Danaos, Author of Nei Kung

We want to make meditation very complicated, but, in reality, meditation is just the practice of *getting out of the way* of a receptive frame of mind. We can open the door to meditation and put ourselves into more receptive states of mind, but when meditation happens, we enter into a kind of weightless state, a suspension of normal consciousness. In that brief stillness, extremely beneficial things happen to our minds and bodies. We feel filled with well-being and tranquility, and this has ripple effects throughout the body.

For today, try not to worry about technique. This morning, sit in silence and let the silence be your teacher. Bring your mindfulness to bear on this present moment, and you will find the right lesson waiting for you.

Sync Body, Mind, and Environment

When I become conscious of what cognitive loops my brain is running, I then focus on how these loops feel physiologically inside my body. . . . Neuronal loops (circuits) of fear, anxiety or anger, can be triggered by all sorts of different stimulation. But once triggered, these different emotions produce a predictable physiological response that you can train yourself to consciously observe.

Jill Bolte Taylor, Neuroanatomist, Author of My Stroke of Insight

The body and the mind are not separate entities, nor is the body-mind separate from its surroundings. We can describe consciousness as a triangle leading from the brain to the body to the environment. When stress arises, mindfulness practice acts as a synchronizer, getting these three nodes into alignment. Mindfulness also slows down the chaotic flow of energy between these centers and eliminates spurious and deleterious signals.

This morning, do your mindfulness practice in a stressful situation. Perhaps you could meditate during the worst traffic of your commute or when you first sit down at your desk. You don't need to drop everything. Mindfulness is just paying attention to everything that is happening in your body, in your mind, and in your environment. You will find that simply paying attention almost magically brings you into a calmer state.

Cultivating Receptivity

Lift up your heads, O ye gates; And be lifted up,
O ancient doors, That the King of glory may come in!

Psalm 24:7

Waking consciousness has two movements or directions, one active and the other receptive. One direction seeks to control the surround, the other to understand it. Most of us have an overdeveloped active mind and an underdeveloped receptive mind. The goal of mindfulness practice is to increase the listening, receptive mind, to increase our capacity for understanding. One way to accomplish this increased receptivity is to think of opening the senses and opening the mental space. The cramped, crowded confines of the mind grow more expansive when we resolve to be fully present to our inner and outer sensorium.

If you are having difficulty with mindfulness this morning, try going for a walk for as little as ten or twenty minutes. Walking makes mindfulness practice easy since it gives the mind a task to accomplish. As you walk, try to pay attention to each and every step, to every bird, flower, and tree. If you are walking in an urban setting, try not to get too caught up in looking at advertisements and shop windows. You will find that mindfulness comes easily.

Craving the Monastic Life

Divine grace has such a natural transforming influence that the devotee need not renounce anything forcibly. . . . Immersed in love, the true devotee is always flooded with Divine ecstasy, and material trifles lose their power and significance.

Baba Lokenath, Hindu Saint

Have you ever wanted to renounce the rat race and turn to the robes and paraphernalia of the ascetic monk for true inner peace? Consider this: Any monk of any tradition will tell you that the robes do not tame an unruly mind and can even induce new troubles and temptations. Sannyasins (renunciates) and laypeople have different lifestyles, but they struggle internally with the same difficulties and must work with the same inner architecture. The real work must begin in the heart and radiate outward: The robes signify this inner change and not the other way around.

Perhaps at some point in the past you have desired a monastic vocation for yourself. Maybe you have criticized and berated yourself for not achieving such a state, or for not being *more spiritual*. Take a few minutes to offer yourself forgiveness for the past, and say to yourself, "My station in life right now is enough and more than enough. I am grateful for the life and lifestyle that I have. I will seek liberation in my own life and time."

Orient Yourself with Your Center

Both to delight in and to be pained by the things that we ought;
this is the right education.

Aristotle, Ancient Greek Philosopher

A good compass points to the magnetic north, but this information is of no use without a good map and a skilled orienteer. In the moral life, we can get ourselves turned around by failing to understand the landscape in which we live, both at the microlevel of interpersonal relations and at the macrolevel of societies and nations. Mindfulness practice helps us understand the terrain in which we live, to be aware of the forces at work in each situation in which we find ourselves. It also helps us find the moral *magnetic north*, which is the pull of conscience or intuition guiding us in one direction or another.

Perhaps you are feeling pulled in more than one direction in your life. Mindfulness can help center you before making any rash decisions. Find the still, calm part of yourself in your heart center. Stay with this silence as long as you are able. Repeat this practice at repeated intervals over several days. Then evaluate any possible decisions as to whether they will help you maintain a calm center or will make it more difficult to maintain a calm center.

Redirect Your Mind

There is always reaction in our life—that is, when we live in the external consciousness, there is always reaction. Suffering is caused by reaction. Our miseries, our pains, our complaints, our doubts, our troubles, our disillusionments, our despair, have always been caused by the outer consciousness.

Swami Prakashananda, Founder and Acharya of Chinmaya Mission of Trinidad and Tobago

Like a loyal dog, the practical, waking consciousness just wants to be helpful. It is directed toward problem solving. When presented with boredom, it will say, "Hey, look at this. I can fix that!" The same goes for other negative states. And yet these *solutions* are actually tangles or complications that compound the problem. Through mindfulness, we must somehow tell the waking consciousness to relax, that all is well, that it can take a break.

This morning, practice mindfulness while doing some mundane task like washing the dishes or getting dressed. Note that multiple lines of thought will emerge that have nothing to do with the task at hand. Redirect the chattering mind through the use of a simple phrase like *It's okay. I've got this*. Then gently return your attention to the awareness of the present moment.

Meditation on Death

Were you to live three thousand years, or even thirty thousand,
remember that the sole life which a man can lose is that which he is
living at the moment; and furthermore, that he can have no other
life except the one he loses.

Marcus Aurelius, Roman Emperor, Philosopher

All of us live on a wisp of time, a thin slip of existence on the brink of the abyss. So we should number our days and ask that we be granted a vision of our mortality. Meditation on death was one of the primary classical disciplines in both the East and the West, and yet today we often think we are too high-minded, too *optimistic* to contemplate death. Our failure to successfully deal with mortality is a primary driver of our narcissism and nihilism.

Ponder for a few moments that this life and everything in it will come to an end. This need not be morbid or depressing: Just acknowledge this as a concrete fact, an inevitability. Given this finitude, how do you want to spend the limited time that you have available? Resolve on this new day to live each moment to the fullest, to savor each and every second, and to express the highest ideals that you have within you.

Find the Love Within You

Love is the unifying and propagating principle of the cosmos. It shows us our oneness, binds and entwines us inextricably in one another's lives. Manifesting both physically and spiritually, it is the meeting of hearts, of minds, bodies, and souls. It is the highest expression of affinity. It impels us to acts of passion and compassion, and it is also the reward for such acts.

Thomas Ashley-Farrand, Hindu Acharya

When we think about love, we often think of it as something that we *do* rather than something that comes before us and into which we *enter*. If we think of love as the matrix, lattice, or womb into which we are born, it causes us to think of love as the base condition or default setting of the universe. Acts of cruelty can then be properly seen as the aberrations that they are rather than the natural condition of humankind. When we live in love and strive for it, we return to our origins as beings born of the Mother of the Universe.

Take a few minutes to center yourself in the quiet stillness of this morning. Allow your breath to rise and fall gently and draw your attention to your breath. You may concentrate either on the heart center or on the point between the brows. Now see yourself suffused with love, which may appear as a roseate glow. Allow all stress, tension, and worry to dissolve into the cosmic love that surrounds you throughout this day.

Push Past Limits

*Very truly, I tell you, unless a grain of wheat falls into the earth and dies,
it remains just a single grain; but if it dies, it bears much fruit.*

John 12:24

When we feel uninspired in life, as though nothing is going right, it is often because we are holding something back. We all have a tendency to hedge our bets, to not put forth a full effort. Even when we do exert ourselves in some area of life, we tend to set limits ahead of time. The underlying belief is that the universe is not a trustworthy place, and we cannot afford to give our best. But amazing things only begin to happen when we give beyond reason and push past our own limits without regard for the results.

Think of a time when you put forth a good effort and fell flat on your face. Did this cause you to go into a defensive crouch in some area of your life? What would it take to get you to go out there and try again? This morning, as the new day dawns, give yourself permission to make a fresh start. Choose an area where your progress has been stymied and put forth an unreasonable amount of energy in tackling the problem.

Reboot Your Mind

The most meaningless trouble is caused by holding to ready-made ideas. It happens if someone does not return to the zero point, or if someone does not know the value of the zero point. The truth of Tao is the zero point, the point where anything can be produced. It gives birth to all things.

Hua-Ching Ni, Taoist Master

At the end of the class, the teacher wipes the board clean so that it is prepared for the next lesson. The short-order cook uses spare moments to clear the workstation so that future orders will go smoothly. After installing new software, the office worker reboots the machine so that the changes take effect. In the same way, the mind functions best when it has been given a chance to start over again. The meditator seeks to return the mind to a clear state so that it will be ready for the day's activities.

As you meditate this morning, see the thoughts arising like water coming out of a fountain. In order to reset your mind, do not inquire into the thoughts. Pay more attention to the empty spaces between the thoughts. Try to lengthen those empty spaces, those silences. Strive to get to the point where there is more quiet than noise. Dwell there for as long as you can.

Spiritual Journaling

While planning action steps and a time line to reach your goals is important,
it is the present moment that guides thoughts and actions at another level,
by way of synchronicity: unexpected connections rather than careful plans,
sudden leaps rather than deliberate steps.

Cheryl Grace, Feng Shui Consultant

Spiritual journaling can be a good way to connect what you thought were completely unrelated parts of your life. You might see that how you deal with a colleague at work is related to an episode from childhood, or you might have an insight about how to stop procrastinating. In short, you never know what you will find when you first put your pen to a blank page. If the devil is in the details, so is the divine.

A good practice for spiritual journaling is to write quickly, off the top of your head, for no more than three pages, or thirty minutes. This practice should not feel heavy, depressing, or arduous. If you have nothing to say, just write down your grocery list. At the end of the practice, make a note to yourself of any action items and then shred and recycle the pages.

Permission Slip for Self-Care

*It is more important for you to keep the resolutions
you have already made than to go on and make noble ones.*

Seneca, Philosopher

Most of us already have a pretty good idea of the activities in life that make us happy, sane, and well adjusted: It's just that we shortchange ourselves by compromising on self-care. Usually exercise, meditation, and a good diet are the first things to go out the window when a stressful situation arises. Of course, this only makes matters worse as our physical and mental health deteriorate. To get things back on the right track, we have to begin with today and not with self-blame and self-doubt connected to the past. Each day is a new chance to start anew, to live the life that we most want to live.

As this day begins, give yourself permission to care about your mind and body. Your physical condition is not everything, and the body is only a vehicle, but feeling good makes it easier for you to care about yourself and others. This morning, try doing a few yoga asanas or your favorite form of exercise. Take a long lunch break and sneak some time outdoors. See yourself becoming more serene and loving as you take care of your physical condition.

Get to Know Your Motivations

What we manage to do each time we win a victory is not so much to secure change once and for all, but rather to create new terrains for struggle.

Angela Y. Davis, Scholar, Activist

The ego craves solidity in a world of flux, permanence in a world of change, product in a world of process. Meditation conditions the mind to appreciate the ephemeral, to welcome the fleeting with gratitude, to see the beauty in a broken world. And yet meditative practice seeks justice, not justice from above, but justice from below, in this place and time. To be aware is to care for the marginalized in society: the prisoner, the immigrant, and the outcast.

Take a few moments now to analyze your motivations for meditating. Do you seek to enhance your concentration or psychic ability? Do you crave exalted spiritual states? Are you looking for wealth and fame? Try for just a little while to let go of these motivations and to open yourself to whatever arises.

Living in Line with Your Goals

Faced with what is right, to leave it undone shows a lack of courage.

Confucius, Philosopher

The general haste of our lives, together with the lack of discipline and fore-sight entailed by such fraught activity, leads to confusion and error. We do not see the way to live because we are too busy keeping up with the tread-mill of contemporary life. And yet we can use this busyness as an excuse for not doing what we know we should. In order to live better lives, we must slow down and pay closer attention to our actions and their conse-quences. We must learn to do things right the first time rather than having to complete a lot of rear-guard correctives.

This morning, spend a few minutes in silence. When you are ready, ask yourself, "What is my goal in this life?" Inquire further to ask, "Will my actions today be directed toward my life's goal?" If the answer is no, think about some possible adjustments you could make. If the answer is yes, go serenely forward and confidently take each step with great care and inten-tionality. At the same time, realize that goal setting can be unrealistic and lead to harsh self-judgment. In some cases, it can be better to let go of the whole exercise.

Peace As Practice

One does not need buildings, money, power, or status to practice the Art of Peace. Heaven is right where you are standing, and that is the place to train.

Morihei Ueshiba, Founder of Aikido

The temptation is always to think you can only obtain peace once you are surrounded by favorable conditions, by good and kind people, by material plenty. You might also think you have to have special certifications and positions of power in order to make society more peaceful. And yet, this mentality always pushes peace off into the future, off into some unattainable realm. If peace is to become a reality, it will have to be peace in this world, right in the places where you live each day. Peace can be achieved through good thoughts and good actions.

Take several minutes to inwardly cultivate feelings of peace and harmony for all beings. After meditating in this way for as much time as you have, make a list of two or three things you can do today to make the world a more peaceful place. This could be as simple as resolving not to get angry or donating to a favorite charity. As you go about this day, complete each tiny act with universal love and benevolence.

ONE DOES NOT NEED
BUILDINGS, MONEY, POWER,
OR STATUS TO PRACTICE THE

Art of Peace.

HEAVEN IS RIGHT
WHERE YOU ARE STANDING,
AND THAT IS THE PLACE TO TRAIN.

—MORIHEI UESHIBA,
FOUNDER OF AIKIDO

Slow Down to ⅔ Pace

Success can only be one ingredient in happiness, and it is too dearly purchased if all the other ingredients have been sacrificed to obtain it.

Bertrand Russell, Philosopher

Wanting to *get things done* without regard to the manner in which they are done will certainly kill any prospects for mindfulness practice. We are very good at discovering what needs to be done and when it needs to be done: We are less good at the how. Because we are so focused on the quantity of our achievements, the quality of our experiences get neglected. We rush through life, forgetting to care about the richness that life offers. We forget to care about other people, we forget to care about aesthetic beauty, and we forget to care about our own well-being.

This morning, try doing everything that you would ordinarily do at ⅔ the pace. Drive more slowly, walk more slowly, and talk more slowly. Notice your own reactions to this process, including any fear that might arise from *not getting things done*. See if other people notice the difference and gauge whether their reactions are positive or negative. See if you are able to be more observant and connected while taking life slowly.

Questioning *Happiness*

We control events and events control us. The world keeps our ambitions enticing but slippery. No particular approach to life has unmixed success.

John F. Williams, Philosopher

If we think to ourselves, *Am I really happy*?, we will commit ourselves to a certain torturous exercise that the question entails. A bank of culturally determined assumptions will arise, easy-to-reach yardsticks we might use to answer the question, which immediately turns into a comparison game. We might ask, for example, if we make enough money or have the ideal body weight or have the *right* career or a house in the *right* neighborhood. Or we might make internal comparisons to our lives, say five or ten years ago, asking if we are on an upward or downward trend. The line of questioning about happiness seems destined at best to measure random ups and downs, and, at worst, become a form of self-flagellation.

As your exercise this morning, take a step back from the question, *Am I really happy*? Let go of the assumptions that the question entails. Give yourself the permission to stop comparing yourself, either against others or your own best self. You will find that the comparisons seem to come automatically: Each time they arise, let them go again. Give yourself a brief vacation from the comparison game.

Recover Your Artistry

When we imprison another we must also place one of our own in
prison as a guard. Likewise when we imprison a part of ourselves,
other parts must move into that same dungeon.

Derrick Jensen, Author, Environmental Activist

As the years accumulate, we begin to wear the disappointments and scars of life like merit badges on a sash over our shoulders. We pride ourselves on surviving, which is, indeed, our core evolutionary tendency. And yet, our ancient ancestors did not merely survive. They also painted on cave walls and danced around fires: They made beautiful works of art that survive to this day. We should not let the passage of time entomb us, but instead let that passage become a celebration. We have to make some pigments and get to work on a fitting tribute, a cave painting, to the beautiful things in this life.

As a result of past trauma, you may have let go of some key aspect of your joy in living. Maybe you once loved painting, drawing, dancing, or singing. You were held back because you thought you weren't *good enough*, or you were told that your plans were impractical. This morning, think about something that once gave you joy that you relinquished to please others. Think about some ways to be more mindful of your own need for creative expression and give yourself permission today to honor your inner artist.

Respect Your Power

No one is born hating another person because of the color of his skin, or his background, or his religion. People must learn to hate, and if they can learn to hate, they can be taught to love, for love comes more naturally to the human heart than its opposite.

Nelson Mandela, *South African Anti-Apartheid Revolutionary*

Most of the misery that we face in life is self-caused. Events are good or bad, not in themselves but based on our reactions to them. We can choose to go down the path of resentment and rage, or we can choose to go down the path of reconciliation and recovery. We cannot control the entire world stage, but we can choose how to respond to circumstances as concerned individuals and as members of society. Our choices, no matter how small, ripple outward to affect the whole world, so we should never imagine ourselves to be powerless.

Your life is at the fulcrum, the pivot point, of the balance of so many other lives, human and nonhuman, nearby and far away. Take a few minutes this morning to cultivate a loving attitude of mind and heart. Take a few minutes to imagine in your mind's eye the many places and people that your life touches directly and indirectly. Wish all beings peace as you go about your daily activities, and dedicate each action to the well-being of the world.

Love List

Love is always what awakens both knowledge and volition;
indeed, it is the mother of spirit and reason itself.

Max Scheler, Philosopher

We cannot understand something unless we first care about it. This is true whether we care about another person, about geology, or about fly-fishing. Concern or care must be awakened by love, which gives rise to interest and action. We can then name love as the value of values, that which makes value possible, that which makes caring possible. There are gradations of love, yes, and love can be misguided or wrongly directed, but love still lies at the center of life, making life worthwhile and livable.

Make a list this morning, mentally or on paper, of the things, activities, people, and places that you love. By the end of the exercise, you will have, in very tangible form, a list of the reasons that you have for living. Think of what you can do today to express your love, to deepen it, to increase your contact with the objects of your affections. Return to this list whenever you need a reminder of the good things in life.

I Am You, You Are Me

In this universe . . . what are you to me and what am I to you?
All are like the bubble or the foam of water. The meeting and separation are
in the hands of the lord. . . . No one is independent.

Brahma Vaivarta Purana 16.7–8

All of our conditioning in Western consumer societies is dedicated to the production of a feeling of separateness, of individuality, of duality. This feeling is useful if the goal is to produce a sense of competitiveness and productivity, but it is deleterious if the goal is to produce feelings of peace and harmony. Mindfulness practice helps us realize our innate kinship with other creatures and the Earth so that we do not approach life from a sense of aggression and lack.

As you go through your morning, say silently to yourself as you meet each person or event, "I am you, and you are me." You can say this to yourself when you greet the cashier at the service station, when you see a squirrel run across the lawn, when you look up at the sky. Persevere in this practice throughout the day. See if you notice a change in the tenor of your responses to the world around you.

Truly Experience Your Senses

Once there is perfect self-control, it is no fault to enjoy the beauty of the earth . . . And indeed, the eternal is of one stock with the beautiful.

Plotinus, Ancient Greek Philosopher

The religions of the world have sounded loud alarm bells about the life of the senses since it is supposed that the senses always drag us away from the highest and best. I think that the trouble with sensation is we don't take the trouble to sense deeply enough; we are always gliding instead over the surface of things. We don't see, feel, hear, smell, taste deeply enough, and that is the real tragedy. We never get to the most sublime moment when the temporal and the eternal touch one another.

Take a few minutes this morning to really savor the passing moment. Fix your powers of observation on something captivating in the surround. This could be raindrops migrating down your car windshield, a child playing with a toy, the sound of crickets, the taste of a glass of water. Try to shut out everything but that one sensory experience right in front of you. Attend only to that one thing and hold nothing back, even if it becomes difficult.

Immerse Yourself in Your Surroundings

Lord, you are my lover, / My longing, /
My flowing stream, / My sun, / And I am your reflection.

Mechthild of Magdeburg, Christian Mystic

We normally think of consciousness as having an *inside* and an *outside*. There is the world *out there*, and I am *in here*. Mindfulness practice seeks to eliminate this distinction by having the mind be wholly immersed in the surroundings, so the mind and world are one and the same. We can't help having a conceptual apparatus or mental categories through which we view the world, but we should dispense with them when they have done their work. It should be possible to hold these categories in suspension and encounter the world in a more direct way.

Choose some stark feature of your surroundings, inside or outside. This could be the bare bark of a tree, a white wall, or a cloudy sky, so long as the sight is not too busy. You might instead choose a neutral sound like static or a meditation chime. Attune your senses to that sight or sound, letting all else fade away. Allow the sensation to fill your mind completely so there is no room for any distracting thought. Hold this frame of mind for as long as you are able.

Quiet the Voice of Despair

I am the fire of life that animates the world. I am not to be found in the sky, not to be found in some remote heaven. I live in your midst, and all that lives lives in the midst of me. I am HERE and I am never absent.

Daniel Quinn, Author

Each one of us has a wretched voice inside—the voice of despair—that must be totally conquered in order for peace to flourish. This voice of despair can be extremely subtle and manipulative. It always seeks solace in another place and time that is always depicted as so much more ideal than the present circumstances. It specifies that demands a, b, and c must be met before it will be quiet. As soon as a, b, and c have been met, demands for x, y, and z soon follow. The voice of despair never rests, nor does it recognize itself as despair. Despair is really a kind of alienation, an inability to say, "This place and time are enough and more than enough for me."

This morning, set aside some time to go away to a quiet place for a few minutes. Notice that as soon as you arrive in your sacred space, your mind will immediately find reasons why you cannot afford to take a break. Your thoughts will run to your to-do list, to your family or colleagues who need you, to your e-mail inbox, or text messages. Staying here in this moment will require firm resolve and an ability to say no to restlessness.

Cherish Our Sacred Sun

May the adorable Lord (in the sun), diversely rich in lustre, the immortal and all-wise, listen to my invocations accompanied by sacred hymns. The brown, red and ruddy horses (rays of the sun at dusk, morn, and during the day) draw his chariot of creation. Then His glory is diffused in all regions.

Rig Veda II.10.2

The divine fire has many manifestations. As the sun, it provides heat and light to all living things, making our planet habitable. As the sacred fire, it receives the offerings of humankind, making possible the giving of thanks for Earth's bounty. As the fire of the mind, it makes understanding possible. As the warmth of the body, it allows us to perform austerities for the removal of impurity.

This morning you can see the rays of the sun, the rays of divine blessing, coming through your window: Do not take them for granted. If you are able, try performing sun salutations (surya namaskar). As you do, think about the light of the sun becoming one with the warmth of your own body. Realize that you owe life itself to the sun, the center of our solar system. This is not a metaphor or an abstraction, but it is scientifically true.

Step Outside Yourself

You and I are mirages who perceive themselves, and the sole magical machinery behind the scenes is perception . . . When perception at arbitrarily high levels of abstraction enters the world of physics and when feedback loops galore come into play, then "which" eventually turns into "who."

Douglas Hofstadter, Cognitive Scientist

The human mind, a curious thing, can invent imaginary objects and places. It can navigate through all sorts of unfamiliar places and undertake difficult tasks. It can produce great cruelty and great acts of kindness as well. We habitually push our minds to new feats, but the most difficult acts of mind may be the simplest. Rarely do we allow the mind to just let go, to stop working so hard, to just be. Mindfulness practice allows us to observe the everyday, mundane miracle of our brains interacting with the world.

This morning, observe yourself as if from the third person. Do not say *I* to yourself or about yourself: Say *he*, *she*, *it*, or whatever pronoun you prefer. See your mental monologue as though it does not belong to you (and it doesn't). Regard thoughts as a passing train or a flock of birds. Hold onto this third person perspective as long as you can: for an hour or for the day. See if you are able to be more present to life if you no longer regard yourself as the subject.

Saying No

It's not a doing but an undoing, a giving up, an abandonment of the false belief that there's anyone here to abandon. What else is there to do?

Douglas Harding, Spiritual Teacher

Narratives of success and self-help put a lot of pressure on the average middle-class person to be more and do more, to make a mark on the world, to get rich, to change things, to make a difference, to *disrupt* technology or the market. Some of these narratives are more harmful, others possibly benevolent, but they all encourage frantic activity. And behind all of this activity is supposed to be the innovator, the genius, the individual as brand. The flip side, the dark side of this hyper-optimism, is that the present moment gets trampled in the quest to do more and be more.

No matter how much pressure we put on ourselves, or others put on us, we can always say *no*. We can say *no* to the narrative of success, just as we can say *no* to the salesperson or the missionary at the door. As you go about the day this morning, take some deep breaths and welcome the day in front of you. Let go of the success narratives that tell you that you are not good enough: Just enjoy the morning as it is.

Examining Your Favorite Fix

The self-radiant one operates through these harnessed sevens (five organs of senses and mind and intellect on the spiritual plane)—never failing and ever purifying, and thus safely draws the chariot of inner cosmos.

Sāma Veda VI.V.639

The senses present no danger to the self-gathered person, who yokes together awareness, intellect, and sensation. Disorders and addiction arise when the craving for pleasure gets out of control and overruns the aims of life. Getting on the path to liberation requires not complete denial of the senses but restraint of the senses, putting the life of pleasure into its proper context. Mindfulness practice helps you see clearly the line between harmless enjoyment and self-indulgence. Not only does mindfulness help you see this difference, but it also fortifies the sincere seeker with hidden consolations that make it easier to abstain.

Look this morning, for five or ten minutes, at any addictive behaviors that might be preventing you from engaging in mindful living. This could be a form of self-medication, through drugs or alcohol, or it might be an addiction to food, television, or the Internet. Would you be able to go one day without your favorite fix? Why or why not? Could you perhaps make it through half a day?

Drawing Inspiration

The optimal state of inner experience is one in which there is order in consciousness. . . . The pursuit of a goal brings order in awareness because a person must concentrate attention on the task at hand. . . .
A person who has achieved control over psychic energy . . .
cannot help but grow into a more complex being.

Mihaly Csikszentmihalyi, Psychologist

All of us live at least some parts of our lives completely engaged and immersed in what we are doing. This can often be achieved through some sort of work with the hands like knitting, drawing, or sculpting. Such experiences are satisfying because they require a great amount of technical and mental skill, and yet they also produce a pleasing end product. Not everyone needs to be a great artist or craftsperson, but everyone should have at least one activity that they thoroughly enjoy and can get completely lost in. Once such complete concentration has been attained in one area of life, it can be brought into other areas as well, so that everything ultimately becomes a kind of meditation.

This morning, spend ten minutes or more doing an activity by hand like drawing or coloring. Don't worry about trying to do it *the right way*: Call it *doodling* if it makes you feel better. Keep going at least long enough so you lose track of time, if only for a few seconds. Ignore any self-critical commentary that arises, and feel no need to show your work to others. Perhaps you'll see some ways to bring this same level of creativity and engagement into your everyday life. Or perhaps you'll think of some abandoned project that you could bring back to life, increasing your level of satisfaction and enjoyment.

Practice Refinement

Listen only to the voice which is soundless. Look only on that which is invisible alike to the inner and the outer sense.

Mabel Collins, Theosophist

The mindfulness practitioner harnesses the senses, sharpens them, becomes hyperalert and vigilant, attending to the surfaces until they boil over into higher awareness. The stark reality of the present yields awareness of the divine heart of all things. Mindfulness practitioners cultivate inner peace, and yet they are never satisfied with the tranquility that has arisen so far. They send back the gifts of the spirit to their source, and in this way, the peace and tranquility are transmuted into bliss. This *something else* might be called inner divinity or Buddha nature, and it is called, in some strands of Christianity, entire sanctification. Many see glimpses of it, but few can enter this state and remain.

As you go about your mindfulness practice today, notice any pleasant and peaceful states that arise. Practice sending them away like you would any other distracting thought. You will experience a deepening, a going beyond what you have seen so far. If any feelings of accomplishment arise, let go of these as well. Seek to remain in a state of unknowing. Go deeper into the inner darkness, and do not be afraid.

Listen only
to the voice
which is soundless.
Look only on that
which is invisible
alike to the inner and
the outer sense.

—MABEL COLLINS, THEOSOPHIST

Cultivate Inner and Outer Silence

It is not the rupees that I want. I want nishta (concentrated faith) and saburi (patience combined with courage).

Sai Baba of Shirdi, Hindu Saint

Nothing could be easier than mindfulness practice, since it is nothing more than paying attention. And yet nothing could be harder because we so easily get lost in distractions, either the inner monologue or forms of infotainment. At first, you will be able to stay with the practice for no more than a few minutes at a time, but gradually you will improve your ability to stay centered and aware. This will require great perseverance and effort.

One thing that helps to maintain mindfulness throughout the day is to begin the day with mindfulness, as you are doing now. Try setting a timer for twenty minutes. Sit in that silence and listen as deeply as possible. Try to move the exterior silence into the inner space. Let this be a point of reference for the rest of the day: See if you can cultivate inner silence even in the midst of activity. Cultivate silence in traffic, in line at the store, while brushing your teeth.

Find Your Sacred Word

Let us stand well. Let us stand in awe. Let us be attentive,
that we may present the holy offering in peace.

The Divine Liturgy of Saint John Chrysostom

The work of peace takes great patience and perseverance, but our minds tend to balk at the enormity of the task. Engaging in entertainment and daydreaming is just so much easier than sitting to meditate or working on important projects. Making the Earth and our own lives more peaceful requires not only the ability to transform external circumstances but also the ability to discipline our own minds, which always want to wander. So we must call ourselves back, again and again, to the work of internal and external transformation. The long way seems hopeless at times, but glimmers of truth shine brightly from time to time, giving encouragement.

This morning, before going about your day, spend five to ten minutes looking for a sacred word that will call your mind back to attentiveness. After a few minutes of silence, the word will come to you. It might be something simple like *peace, awake,* or *still.* When you are feeling anxious, repeat the sacred word, and do some deep breathing. It may feel forced at first, but eventually you will be able to put yourself intentionally into a better frame of mind.

Lean Into the Moment

Your state of mind is what is important, not where you are.

Mahabharata

The most luxurious setting will not be satisfying or enjoyable if your mind is in a funk. In the same way, the most rundown lodgings will be perfectly bearable with the right frame of mind. We try so hard to rearrange the scenery, but that strategy doesn't work if the inner disposition rebels. Even when the external conditions are perfectly arranged, that perfection will not last in a changing universe. If we can learn the inner work, the inner alchemy, no circumstance will ever get in the way of peace. Without the inner work, no circumstantial change will make a difference. Even a small dose of mindfulness can make the difference between a good day and a bad day.

This morning, make yourself a promise that no matter how things go today, whether everything goes according to plan or not, you will take a pause every now and then to center yourself and remain in touch with the present moment. Resolve to do your best with the tasks at hand, without regarding the result. Take these first few minutes of the day to lean into the present moment, to feel the thickness of the present. Notice the texture and life of this time and hold in your heart an unreasonable feeling of joy.

Abandon Complaints

The hard core of egotism is difficult to dislodge except rudely. With its departure, the Divine finds at last an unobstructed channel. In vain It seeks to percolate through flinty hearts of selfishness.

Paramahansa Yogananda, Founder of Self-Realization Fellowship

The ego never presents itself as such. It will speak instead of justice, of what is *only right*. The ego, a phantom or byproduct of the mind, has an inherently insecure existence. It seeks to justify itself by claiming to look out for *you*. And so it goes around logging evidence to be used against other people, imagining all sorts of slights and then blowing them out of proportion. The ego is like an internal propaganda machine, and it aims chiefly at promoting division. The more you listen to that voice, the more miserable your life becomes as a chasm divides you more deeply from others.

This morning, on a scribble or scratch pad, write down a few of your mind's most frequent complaints about other people, your job, your city, etc. Then take that sheet of paper and shred it, or better yet, burn it. What would your life look like if you were finally able to leave these complaints behind? It is much more difficult to dislodge the mental complaints than it is to burn the paper, but try mentally surrendering them for a few minutes. Be open to the prospect that the future has more in store for you than the repeated recitation of complaints.

Upright Posture, Sincere Intention

Attainment is not encompassed within four and twenty hours, nor within several settings of the sun. . . . The wings then grow stronger, the flight itself grows longer, and the inner lamp fed on the flame of wisdom remains constantly burning. . . . What is required first of all is that imperturbable aspiration and indomitable Will; then work!

Israel Regardie, Occultist

If the spiritual aspirant has a passion for awakening, for illumination, for insight, then nothing will stop that seeker from moving forward with strength. Without this passion, every effort comes to nothing, the will grows dull, the intellect dim. Properly channeled passion leads quickly to realization. By passion, I do not mean great emotion, but great intensity of will. This intensity of will must be put into keeping the mind securely focused on the present moment. Without intensity, mindfulness is just another buzzword, just another meaningless trope. The word *patience* can be misleading, if by patience we mean just waiting around for something to happen. Apply patience only to circumstances beyond your control while fully exercising those capacities that do lie within your control.

This morning, spend a few minutes focusing on your posture. Sit comfortably with your feet fully touching the floor, or, if you are able, sit in lotus posture or half lotus. Keep your carriage as upright as the physical condition of your body allows. Allow this expectant, alert body posture to carry over into your mental attitude. Do five to ten minutes of silent listening as though you expect something to happen!

Zoom Out

*While cosmic wisdom understands all things are just and good,
intelligence may find injustice here, and justice somewhere else.*

Heraclitus, Ancient Greek Philosopher

If we could see all of space and time under the aspect of eternity, we would
be capable of seeing the infinite perfection of the universe. But because
we live in our small, compartmentalized lives, we think that we have *good*
and *bad* days. We think the whole world hinges on whether or not the line is
long for buying a cup of coffee in the morning. All the while, other human
beings are living in refugee camps and worrying about their next meal.
Compassion demands that we broaden our perspective, not only to include our human neighbors, but nonhuman life as well. We can learn from
science and philosophy the cosmic vision of seeing all of human history as a
blip in time, and, from that perspective, we gain freedom from the troubles
of the here and now. The feeling of release enables us to care more deeply
about others.

With your eyes closed, imagine your own life as it appears this morning.
Then *zoom out* to situate your own life within the context of your nation.
Then imagine how you fit into global society. Then imagine how you fit into
the biotic community, the collective of all living things. Then see how you
fit into geologic time and the history of the planet. Although it may be

difficult, think about all you know about the universe and its origins. Gradually come back down to everyday consciousness, and see if your perspective has shifted.

You Are Not the Doer

Reality is simply loss of the ego. Destroy the ego by seeking its identity. Because the ego has no real existence, it will automatically vanish, and Reality will shine forth by itself in all its glory.

Ramana Maharshi, Hindu Saint

Our minds want to complicate everything, to make the business of life a tug of war between competing priorities. The mind loves complexity and will not readily settle down to do something simple. The simplest thing of all, and therefore the most difficult, is to pay attention, to observe, to listen. Entering into the space of receptivity would be the most beneficial thing that the mind can do for us, and yet that is exactly what it most resists. So we must enter into deliberate training to get the mind to surrender and sit still. It will summon its allies, the emotions, to instill panic or anger, but we must persist in the practice until the great quiet dawns.

Before beginning the day, take five or ten minutes to realize that you are not the doer because *you* are a bundle of various processes, such as emotion, sensation, etc. Because there is no self behind these processes, there is no ego. Instead, regard God or the cosmos as the doer. You are not separate from this God or this cosmos; therefore, there is no duality. You do not need to prove yourself or be more than you are, since you are already united with the whole. Every time the sense of separation arises, gently bring the mind back to the vision of the whole. You don't have to *give up* anything because there is nothing to be surrendered in the first place.

Fine-Tuning Yourself

When harmlessness is established in the mind, it radiates outward
just as fragrance pours out of a flower. . . . In the same way,
the mind transmits its kindliness to the hands and feet,
and through them it brings about harmlessness.

Jnaneshwari *13.304, 308*

Picture an instrument, say a guitar, going out of tune. Even the humidity in the air and the changes in temperature will cause the strings to expand or contract slightly, the tuning pegs to turn, and the wood to swell or buckle by miniscule increments. Just sitting still, the guitar goes out of tune. The musician must tune the instrument, either by ear or with the aid of an electronic tuner. Or the musician can find an instrument that has already been tuned and tune the guitar in that manner. Once the instrument has been tuned, the possibility of making good music arises. Of course, the musician will still have to be skilled, but without good tuning, skill doesn't matter.

In the same way, mindfulness or meditation practice tunes the instrument of the body and mind. The body and mind, it should be *noted* (ha!), are not the music, not the main event, but they are only the instrument through which the *music* of divinity flows. To tune your instrument this morning, allow yourself to be fully in touch with the present moment, getting rid of the sharps and flats of egotism and ignorance. Without this tuning, no achievement in life makes any difference: It will not ring true; it will not be harmonious with the whole. The discordant notes have their place, but only within the context of the greater work.

Stop Escaping

*One of the metaphors for ego is a cocoon. We stay
in our cocoon because we're afraid—we're afraid of our feelings. . . .
We're afraid of what might come at us. . . . But what the Buddha observed is
that . . . trying to find zones of safety creates terrible suffering.*

Pema Chödrön, Buddhist Nun, Acharya

We spend most of our lives trying to escape from something. We try to escape from everyday boredom, from economic insecurity, from physical threats, and from emotional discomfort. These ceaseless attempts at escape create a kind of debt in that we are not living in reality but in some sort of make-believe world where the scary things can't get to us. That means that our efforts are shunted aside, into this parallel reality, instead of going into this real world right in front of us. Of course, this tends to exacerbate the problem rather than making it go away, sapping much-needed resources.

Think of a time when you have been really afraid of something. When the bad, scary thing really happened, was it as bad as you thought it would be? Now think about what you might fear or want to avoid right now. Is it possible that the threat is not as great as you imagine it to be? What would happen if you just let the scary thing happen? Or what would happen if you took some small step toward facing the big, scary thing? See if you can live in the fear and get more comfortable with it this morning.

Undoing Negative Self-Talk

A teaspoon of salt would make a glass of water difficult to drink, but the same teaspoonful dropped in a freshwater lake would make no difference to the taste. In the same way, space created around intense experiences can create a felt sense of diluting their intensity.

Mark Williams, Psychologist

Oftentimes when we mentally rehash the same scenes, the same lines, over and over again, the kernel of experience that originally produced the negative internal dialogue gets distorted into something bigger and more crushing than it ever was in its original context. In order to get our negative experiences to go back down to size, we have to look at them very carefully, to ask what is actually happening or has actually happened. The perceived threat must be seen for what it is, and not through the prism of emotional distortion. This is not to say that we should become automatons, devoid of any feeling: Rather, we must see clearly and feel deeply, in line with the truth of the hurtful moment. Negative experience will not release its hold on the psyche until it has been noticed and felt. Once recognized in its exactness and specificity, the negative experience will become forgettable.

For the next few minutes, look at one of your common phrases of self-talk. It might be *No one cares about me*, or *[So-and-so] takes advantage of me*, or *Nothing I do makes any difference*. Then look at the conditions that give rise to the negative talk. They could be as simple as someone cutting you off in traffic or a bill that is larger than you expected. As soon as you notice the disconnect between the occasion and the reaction, you will be on your way to freedom from the negative state of mind.

Cooperation and Commitment

Most of the problems that we confront day to day are essentially man-made [sic]. They are unnecessary. . . . All these man-made problems ultimately derive from dividing the world in this way: "us" versus "them." We think to ourselves, "We matter; they don't." As a result, we disregard the welfare of others, at times even exploiting and cheating them.

His Holiness the XIVth Dalai Lama

A tribal mindset prevents humanity from working together to solve the biggest problems that we face: climate change, environmental degradation, mass extinction, rampant inequality, war and terrorism, and economic inequality. These problems require unprecedented levels of cooperation and commitment in order to secure a decent future for the planet and its inhabitants. In order for solutions to emerge, we must act in constructive ways. In order for constructive action to be possible, we have to stop carving up the world into little fiefdoms based on religion, ethnicity, nationality, gender, sexual orientation, ability, and the like. We have to begin thinking of ourselves as belonging to the larger orders of nature, as mammalian creatures dependent on a supportive ecosystem, as social animals dependent upon one another.

This morning, as you greet the rising sun, say a quiet word of thanks for the benefits that you receive from a habitable atmosphere and potable

Most of the
problems that we
confront day to day
are essentially man-made [*sic*].

They are unnecessary. . . .
All these man-made problems ultimately
derive from dividing the world in this way:
"us" versus "them."
We think to ourselves,
"We matter; they don't."

As a result, we disregard the
welfare of others, at times even
exploiting and cheating them.

—HIS HOLINESS
THE XIV_{TH} DALAI LAMA

food and water. Say thanks for the people who have inspired you along the way. Say thanks for the good things about your present situation, even if it seems difficult. Resolve this day to make the world more hospitable, kind, and just. Resolve to think of yourself as belonging to nature rather than standing apart from it. Realize that not even your thoughts and dreams ultimately belong to you, as they came from the world and return to it again.

Delve Into Your Messy Places

Weeding is a mindfulness meditation, one that takes patience and love. . . .
Risking the tangle of our garden, we enter the terrain of our inner landscape
as well. There, reflected in the tangle of our garden, lie the knotted up
thoughts and feelings of our minds—stories we tell ourselves over and over
causing ourselves, and others, to suffer.

Zachiah Murray, Zen Gardener

We tend to avoid the messy parts of our lives, but these messy places are exactly where the most growth can be found. The stack of unopened bills might hide the key to financial discipline. The friend you haven't called may have the word you need to hear. The overdue library books might hold an unwritten article or chapter. And yet we shy away from these messy places, partly out of simple laziness but also out of a fear of change. As much as we hate some aspects of our present realities, we hate the unknown even more. To go into those messy places is to risk having to do something about our complaints.

If you are feeling stuck in some part of your life right now, ask yourself for a few minutes, "What have I left undone?" Make a list of a few things, even if they seem trivial or unrelated. Over the next day or two, attend to some of those neglected tasks. You may find a hidden blessing waiting for you in the thing that you didn't want to do.

Stop the Panic

The more you can cultivate a sense of compassion encompassing both your self and other creatures, the easier it will be—not easy, but easier— to deal with pain of any kind. With compassion, we can deal more mindfully, and more skillfully, with pain—whether mental or physical.

David Harp, Meditation and Harmonica Teacher

Having studied and read widely doesn't often help much with mindfulness practice: Oftentimes it just ratchets up the complexity of the justifications that we have for not doing the work. It is much easier to blame the mass media or society or the billionaire class for our fast-paced lives than it is to just admit why we're not doing meditation or practicing mindfulness: *I'm not doing the practice because I'm afraid that if I stop or slow down, even for a few minutes, my world will fall apart. I'm not doing the practice because it hurts too much to take a long, hard look at my own life. I'm not doing the practice because I don't want to see the ugliness in human behavior or all of the hurt in the world.* Now we're getting somewhere.

Our thoughts have a certain momentum, a centrifugal force that can be quite powerful. If your thoughts are racing this morning, to the point where it is difficult to keep reading this brief reflection, try taking some deep breaths. Ask yourself why you started reading this book in the first place. Were you looking for comfort, for peace, for guidance? Give yourself permission today to live mindfully. When you are tempted to go back to frantic activity, think of the goals that motivated you to want to learn about mindfulness in the first place.

Reject Labels with "Not This, Not This"

We train ourselves to use mindfulness to focus on the simple cognitive aspects of perception without going beyond them into judgments and interpretations. We remind ourselves that conceptual proliferation gets in the way of clear perception and always strive to perceive things impartially.

Bhante Gunaratana, Founding Abbot of the Bhavana Society

Mindfulness happens when we deliberately strip away layers of internal talk, of noise, and concentrate on direct experience. Most people do not directly experience the world very much of the time. A barrage of labels keeps the world at bay. We prefer to classify people, things, and experiences. We do this so frequently and so quickly that we barely register our categorizations. These categories seem innocuous enough, but they prevent us from experiencing anything new or surprising. We reduce the new, the novel, to the familiar and known through these categories, thereby depriving ourselves of the moment's freedom and freshness. The world comes to seem leftover and familiar, as exciting as a cardboard box left out in the rain.

To get the mind to backtrack, to let go of its tendency to label, try the yogic technique of saying *not this, not this*, whenever a mental construct arises. Do this for five to ten minutes while seated in your meditation space, and then keep working with this practice throughout the day. Notice any preformed opinions that you may have about the people and situations in your life. Let go of your predetermined labels and try to experience things firsthand once again. If any new labels arise, reject these as well by saying, *not this.* Persevere in this practice as long and as often as possible.

Don't Be a Know-It-All

The skillful musician plays and is played, the skillful surfer surfs the wave and is waved, the artful teacher teaches and is taught; the skillful musician becomes the music, the surfer becomes the wave, and the teacher becomes teaching. Compassion . . . requires the skillful means that becomes second nature to us and issues forth in natural and spontaneous ways.

David Jones, Philosopher

Mindfulness can be expressed in a careful way of doing things, in a certain way of giving the task breathing room, of letting the doing be done in us. In order to step into this mindful action, we must step back from the self-centered approach. (When I say *self-centered*, I mean the belief that I have the answers and I know what I'm doing.) Stepping back from this approach, we allow the materials, the tools, and our collaborators to speak for themselves and act for themselves. We take time to notice and listen, something that is absent from the self-centered approach. This way of action can be much more fulfilling and engaging than the self-centered way, but it is also more difficult in that it asks us to move into uncomfortable spaces of unknowing.

Oftentimes the ego perspective or the self-centered approach manifests itself as a sort of know-it-all voice, which can be expressed out loud or mentally. Do you have such a voice? Take a few minutes to think about it. Maybe you stepped on someone's toes by insulting their intelligence. See if you can learn to recognize this egotistical voice, and, the next time it arises, pay very close attention to it, but do not allow it to take hold of your will to speak or act.

Get Unstuck

Only uncertainty can provide information . . . Put even more directly,
uncertainty is information. *If you are already certain about a given fact,*
no information is communicated to you.

Chuck Easttom, Cryptologist

A car stuck in the mud will spin its wheels when the driver presses the accelerator. If you have ever been in that situation, you know that the temptation is strong to keep stomping on the pedal, as though more of the same could free the tire. The more effective way to free the tire is to place sticks or rocks underneath the tire so that it can gain some traction. Then, by easing forward slowly, the car can get out of the mud. So it is with our own minds. We can spin our wheels in the mud of our own delusions, our own repetitive narration about the world. Only the introduction of new content, a new way of seeing things, can free our stuck minds from the loop of sameness.

This morning, as you sit silently for a few minutes, notice the stream of thoughts as they arise. Dismiss each thought as it appears. Notice that the mind can be very tricky in couching its dialogue in a pious or wise-sounding voice, hoping that you won't notice that it is feeding you the same lines in a different guise. Thoroughly reject all interior monologue as it arises through a sort of mental unclenching. Allow yourself to remain in a state of unknowing for as long as you can maintain it.

Think Just in This Moment

Will is developed by the power of attention. It can only be gained to the extent that we do not give ourselves over to entertainment and self-indulgence. Desire fragments the will and scatters it into the outer world. True will relinquishes desire, recognizing that desire arises from an external compulsion.

David Frawley, Hindu Pandit

In order to have the pleasure of appreciating beauty, of living in an authentic way, of opening to our truest selves, we must also have the pain of holding steadfastly to the present moment, of letting go of addictions, and of dropping the false personas that hinder our development. We cannot have it both ways. Tradeoffs must be made in the quest to live more mindfully. Some busyness will have to go. Some *harmless* diversions will have to go. The mental preoccupations will have to go. None of this is easy work, and it can take years. Indeed, the Eastern philosophies maintain that this work takes lifetimes, so that the process of purification can be brought to its full conclusion.

All of this hard work can be made lighter by focusing only on the task at hand. You have a few minutes of tranquility at the beginning of the day. Just for this moment, let go of all desire. Just for this moment, sit quietly and observe your breath. Just for this moment, stay completely in touch with this place and time. Tell yourself that you can return to your normal mode of being as soon as your time of meditation has ended. Know that you can gradually move your consciousness into a state of inner renunciation over the weeks and months ahead.

Good Qualities

The transitoriness of our existence in no way makes it meaningless.
But it does constitute our responsibleness; for everything hinges upon our
realizing the essentially transitory possibilities. . . .
At any moment, man [sic] must decide, for better or for worse,
what will be the monument of his [sic] existence.

Viktor E. Frankl, Neurologist, Holocaust Survivor

Each of us, as individuals, does not actually choose whether we will *change the world.* Every life is connected with all of the others, and each life affects the whole as the impact of each action radiates outward. So we all *change the world* just by living our daily lives: The only choice we have in the matter is what the exact nature of our impact will be. Given the short span of life and the limitations we all face, we should strive to make our choices count to the greatest degree possible. At the same time, we should be wary of the success narratives that suggest life has to do with *producing* as much as possible. We should look to becoming more patient, understanding, and compassionate people rather than just trying to build a more impressive résumé.

As you begin your day this morning, make a list, on paper or in your head, of the qualities that you would like to embody in your day-to-day interactions. You might think about kindness, courage, sympathy, or any number of good characteristics that mean something to you personally. When you have finished with your list, think about the obstacles or hindrances that might arise as you struggle to live in a mindful way. Think about how you will address the challenging situations that you face today while remembering your listed good qualities.

Simplify Your Life

*The most striking thing about modern industry
is that it requires so much and accomplishes so little.*

E.F. Schumacher, Economist

For all of our supposed sophistication as denizens of the twenty-first century, the needs of humankind have not changed: We still need clean water and breathable air, good food to eat, and clothes on our backs. Likewise, the desires of humankind have not changed in all of recorded history: People still want to be famous and wealthy. They still want a variety of pleasures and luxuries. What has changed is the capacity to devour the Earth at ever more alarming rates and further impoverish the many for the profit of the few. It may seem crazy or naïve, but I think mindfulness can do something about that. Mindfulness can get people, especially those of us living in wealthy, *first-world* nations, to take a long, hard look at our habits and ask if we really need more manufactured stuff, if our lifestyles are really making us happy.

What if we could subtract more stuff and actually be happier? What if we could do less and enjoy life more? Right now, in five or ten minutes, think of five material possessions that you no longer need in your life. Similarly, think of five activities that you can do without. This morning and for the rest of the day, think of ways you can simplify your life so you spend less time in frantic activity and more time in quiet contemplation. You need not tell anyone about your plans: Be mindful of the fact that others may not understand and may criticize your decisions.

Value Relationships
over Ideology

Living selflessly does not mean that you don't have a healthy sense of your unique qualities as a human being, or that you don't have the ego needed to function in the world. It means that you are not limited by a narrow or rigid view of self. You are no longer dominated by the ego.

Ellen Birx, Cofounder of New River Zen Community

The paradox of living as a human being is that we must have a worldview in order to live as productive members of society, and yet these belief systems can be challenged greatly by unfolding events. We are forced, by our nature as incarnate beings, to have religious, political, ethical, and aesthetic considerations that we bring to bear on our decision-making. These beliefs color our every experience, and yet we cannot readily cast them aside. Mindfulness does not actually *clear the slate* of preexisting values: It just helps us to be more aware of the biases and predilections that we bring to our experiences. Rather than taking these beliefs as given, we see their contingent, provisional nature.

Perhaps your worldview, an aspect of your political or religious beliefs, for example, gets in the way of some of your relationships. This morning, as you sit mindfully, can you hold those beliefs in suspension for a few min-

$\mathcal{L}$iving selflessly
does not mean that
you don't have a healthy
sense of your unique qualities
as a human being, or that you
don't have the ego needed to
function in the world. It means
that you are not limited by a
narrow or rigid view of self.
You are no longer
dominated by the ego.

—ELLEN BIRX, COFOUNDER
OF NEW RIVER ZEN
COMMUNITY

utes? Not to say that you disavow them, but that you soften your grip on your ideology for a short time. See if you can make more room in your worldview for contrasting, even conflicting, values. You may see a space of hospitality begin to open, in which you can find a place of compassion and kindness for others, even if you vehemently disagree with their beliefs.

Take One Step Toward Goals

Lakṣya means goal. Lakṣmī manifests the goal, every aim in existence. What our goals are, are what we value; that which we value is our wealth. And it is in this sense that Lakṣmī is the Goddess of Wealth, our goals, our values, our aspirations.

Swami Satyananda Saraswati, Hindu Guru

Pausing to reflect has become a *sin* of our contemporary time in the perverse logic of consumerism and greed. We *must* keep going: do more, buy more, read more, watch more. We tell ourselves that we will have time for spirituality, for meditation, for exercise (later, always later), but the kicker is that later never comes. So we are bound in the cycle of delaying what we really want to do while always immediately attending to what we don't really want to do. To break this cycle, we have to begin to insert pauses into the day, to stop and think *Is this course of action really going to help me achieve my goals in life?* These pauses may last for a few minutes, for hours, or only for a few seconds. The important thing is to regroup, to get your consciousness onto the same wavelength with the desired state of being.

This morning, as you begin your day, take five or ten minutes to reflect on your goals. Picture your ideal life coming into focus in your mind's eye with as much vividness as possible. Do not despair if your present situation differs greatly from what you envision: Just resolve to take a few small steps today toward making that vision a reality. Even the smallest concrete action taken toward a specific goal will put your mind at ease and help you remain fully connected to the present.

Care for Your Mind,
Care for Others

How do you get an empathic child? You get an empathic child not by trying to teach the child and admonish the child to be empathic, you get an empathic child by being empathic with the child. The child's understanding of relationships can only be from the relationships he's [sic] experienced.

L. Alan Sroufe, Child Psychologist

In the West, we have inherited a feeble and narrow model of the mind in which each person has a separate Jell-O mold of a brain, disconnected from all other brains, and therefore from all other persons. A more accurate and responsible view looks at the mind as inherently social and interconnected, with each separate *mind* actually a node in a larger network, encompassing not only other knowers but anything that might be known. Because the mind belongs to this larger web of all entities, what affects one mind will affect the entire network. Caring for one another is so important because it is ultimately about caring for the whole Earth. The entire array of beings—animal, vegetable, and mineral—takes delight whenever one being is respected and is diminished whenever one being suffers.

As you begin your day, notice that your thoughts do not begin or end with you. You are merely the channel through which your thoughts and feelings flow. You can direct that flow in one way or another, but you cannot stop and start it. You can move into more positive or negative states of mind, moving from the depths of despair to the heights of bliss, but you are bound by nature to have states of mind. Resolve this day to move your mind in buoyant and light feelings of peace, and move away from the heavy and dark feelings of animosity and anger. Your intentions have a powerful effect on the state of mind that comes to you.

When You Feel Uninspired

The obstacles in our way are only two, though caused in various ways, namely, dullness and distraction (avarana and vikshepa). . . . The first step . . . is to be intensely active, so that idleness and laziness are entirely banished from life.

J.C. Chatterji, Indologist

Sometimes our ego draws a bright line between the practical and the spiritual spheres. For example, a person may have a strong life of prayer or meditation but be a disaster professionally, or another person may be extremely successful, materially speaking, but have not an ounce of philosophy or devotion. These strategies are not sustainable and ultimately fail because they represent internal division and wavering consciousness. Only the rare individual can harmonize the practical life with the life of wisdom: Rarer still is the person who sees the course through to its conclusion in what might be called enlightenment.

As you endeavor to begin your day with mindfulness, you may feel uninspired, as though today will be just another repetition of the day before. Bear with this feeling for a minute or two, and observe all of its contours. Notice that this feeling is ultimately about a future that has not yet occurred. Whether this feeling has a lot of truth behind it or a little, resolve to live your life today with as much energy as you can muster. Know that while you may not be able to change everything about your world, you will be better off if you live to the fullest, as that depends on you.

The Life of Your Dreams

*Your evolution is proceeding without flaw. All the experiences you
have ever had have led you to where you now stand. . . . You don't
have to wrestle your destiny to the ground like a big growling bear.
Simply cooperate with what wants to happen.*

Alan Cohen, Inspirational Author

The myth of Sisyphus is a fundamental part of the Western psyche, a sort of martyrdom to the difficult and never-ending. We seem to have a patterned belief that there must be some virtue to sticking with untenable circumstances. These circumstances have the benefit of being familiar, if not comfortable. It can be hard to just walk away and let the stone roll down the hill. To do so would feel irresponsible, reckless—not words that adults are accustomed to accepting.

Think this morning about the ways that you have consigned yourself to an unpleasant fate. Are there ways that hold you back from living like you should? What would happen today if you lived the life of your dreams, if you let go of martyrdom? Before you go into a stream of justifications, sit for a few minutes with the possibility of change. Allow an opening in your consciousness for the genuinely new and different. You don't need to go into fantasy mode: Just awaken to the expectation of a better and more satisfying life.

Letting Go of Control

For the three excellent things be never slack, namely, good thoughts, good words, and good deeds; for the three abominable things be ever slack, namely, bad thoughts, bad words, and bad deeds.

Zend Avesta Part I: THE VENDÎDÂD: Fargard XVIII, Trans. James Darmesteter

Letting go of control, we see that things come and go, everything passes, everything changes. Letting go of control, we release exultation and disappointment. Letting go of control, the course of events becomes less important than the attention that we bring to them. The rare person can step back and observe. The rare person can stop trying to find some advantage. The rare person can become a vessel of goodness. In this person, turmoil has ceased, doubt has ceased, greed has ceased. These people have made life livable for the countless millions.

Think for a moment this morning about what makes you sad and disheartened. Usually behind such feelings lies some expectation about the way that the world is *supposed* to be, what you *deserve*, what is *rightfully* yours. See this attitude in your mind's eye, along with the thoughts and feelings that accompany it. When you are ready, let go of this expectation that things should be a certain way, that things should *work out* in a certain manner. Greet the world the way that it is, and be at peace with whatever that might mean.

Working with Resistance

Accepting what is present within us and in front of us right now creates a space for possibilities. Saying yes *to what is, whether it is an emotion, circumstance, relationship, or physical condition, allows us to breathe, observe, and break free.*

Rev. Carla McClellan, Life Coach, Unity Minister

Those of us who practice meditation may be more susceptible than the general population to magical thinking. When things go wrong, we tend to think that we should have said more mantras, or should have gone to the temple more often, or done more yoga asanas. We can be surprised by the deterioration of our bodies, by the troubles in our relationships, and by the behavior of our peers. We sometimes think that the normal rules don't apply to us, that we can circumvent the cares of life through the supernatural. But the good, dharmic teachings show us how to find freedom *within* the limitations of life and nature, how to make ordinary time work *for* us instead of *against* us. We learn how to be friendlier to our own best selves. This happens chiefly through tuning in to daily disciplines of awareness.

This morning, as you arise to start your day, look for the places of resistance or avoidance within your psyche. Look for the parts of your life that you do not wish to face. Make the effort to observe this resistance and its source. Make sure to be generous today with that uncomfortable situation. Give it more of your time and attention. You don't need to *muscle* through the problem, but you do need to face it directly. Pursue mindful, constructive action, and then let nature take its course.

Move from
Separation to Unity

*Spiritual experience is an experience of aliveness of mind and body
as a unity. Moreover, this experience of unity transcends not only the
separation of mind and body, but also the separation of self and world.
The central awareness in these spiritual moments is a profound sense of
oneness with all, a sense of belonging to the universe as a whole.*

Fritjof Capra, Physicist

If one starts from a position of separation and alienation, from an assumption of fundamental difference and exclusion, no amount of mental or emotional seeking will allow him to return to the point of union. But if one can admit that the sense of alienation is not fundamental, that alienation is derivative and accidental, it becomes possible to think of an underlying unity that goes beyond the categorizations invented by human beings. Our vocabulary fails at a certain point because words are designed to classify, an act of sorting or separation. In order to attain the basic, fundamental bliss, we have to work against the urge to classify and divide, to let things be.

Try to go for a few minutes this morning without labeling your interior or exterior experiences. Forget the adjectives: *What a beautiful morning* or

What a crappy cup of coffee. Then forget the nouns: *table*, *lamp*, and *chair*. Forget the pronouns: *I*, *you*, and *we*. Forget the verbs: *walk, drive, read*, and *shop*. Each time the language comes back, send it away. Pay close attention to the things as they present themselves. Keep your mind very vigilant and sharp by negating each new thought as it arises. Persist in this as long as you can. Then try again.

Concentrate on the Task

When you have a feeling to do a certain constructive thing, go ahead, stick to it and do it, if the heavens fall. Whether the manifestation comes now or not, should not enter into your consciousness at all.

Ascended Master Saint Germain

The mindfulness practitioner works efficiently and lightly, not ponderously ruminating upon every step of the operation. Care taken in the work does not go into thinking excessively about what must be done, but rather into the manual task itself. What is commonly taken as intellectual work—say, designing something on a computer or writing—has a significant manual dimension. The mindfulness practitioner simply trusts that the next step will be there without a lot of premeditation. In this respect, mindfulness practice requires faith. The materials needed will be there when the time comes.

After completing five to ten minutes of silent contemplation, go about your morning routine. Be on guard against excessive mental commentary and invest yourself in the task at hand, paying attention to the process without rumination. If your mind should be drawn into some unrelated matter, gently bring it back into the present moment. See how long you can stay in the flow of the task.

Swim in the Deep End

When such "profound contemplation" has been ripened it is called
"meditation" (Samadhi). . . . [When] the function of the internal organ
is unmoved like the unflickering light of a lamp it is called (Nirvikalpa
Samadhi) "contemplation without recognition of subject and object."

Sreemut Vidyaranya Swami, Hindu Philosopher

Why do we hold so tightly to the illusion of separate existence when it causes nothing but pain? I suppose at the root of this clinging is the fear of the unknown. A beginning swimmer will hold to the wall of the pool rather than go out in the deep end, not knowing that the water will support her weight. In the same way, we cling to the ego, thinking that it protects us, when it actually only diminishes our ability to experience the depths of reality. It takes courage, skill, and practice to let go of the ego nature. It happens in fits and starts, a few minutes at a time, and then a little bit longer and a little longer, until we are comfortable with facing the world as it is. At this point, the illusion of separateness disappears, and we realize our union with everything.

Allow yourself this morning to let go of the comfortable confines of your self-created internal dialogue and allow the *outside* into your notion of self. Take the whole universe for your Self, what you can see and what you can't see. Give up the attitude that you are the doer and understand that you are an instrument of the *whole*. Remain rooted in this *whole* as you go about your everyday activities, and banish the illusion of separation whenever it appears.

Life Is Defined by Change

Surrender is a gentle, humble place. There is no more fighting to get your way . . . only the pain and the truth of your situation. In surrender, we accept what is. We give up our control and by doing it, we give in to something greater than we are. And we can be lifted into the new light, and with it into the new possibility.

Auriela McCarthy, Inspirational Author

Most of us want to know where we are headed, whether we are making progress toward our goals. We like the trajectory to be clearly plotted, for our action items to be arranged in *a, b, c* fashion. But sometimes the universe has other plans for us. Sometimes disaster strikes, sometimes things don't go as planned. Sometimes the picture is murky. We have to work hard to be okay with not knowing, to become more flexible and resilient. Sometimes the disappointing but truest message is *wait and see.*

This morning, you may be feeling anxious about your place in life. Maybe you worry that you are not doing enough, that you are stagnating. Know that life in the world is defined by change and that you couldn't stand still even if you wanted to. Your job for today is to show up, do your work, and be as fully present in the moment as you can manage. Let the rest take care of itself.

Surrender is a gentle, humble place. There is no more fighting to get your way . . . only the pain and the truth of your situation. In surrender, *we accept what is.* We give up our control and by doing it, we give in to something greater than we are. And we can be *lifted* into the new light, and with it *into the new possibility.*

—AURIELA MCCARTHY,
INSPIRATIONAL AUTHOR

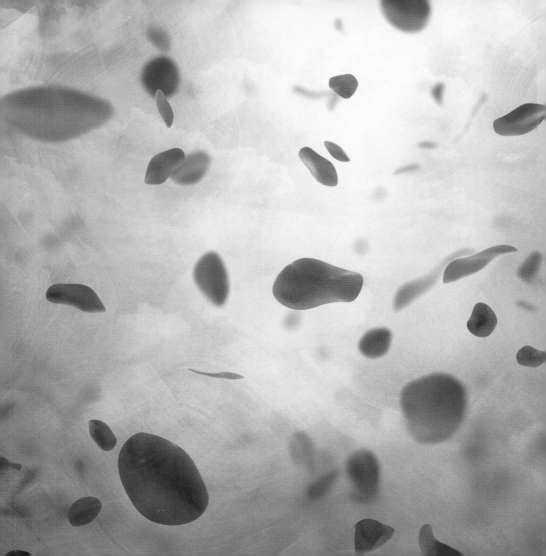

Seek a Placid Disposition

The virtues we cultivate, and the intelligences we acquire,
are so many lamps we light around us, which burn when we sleep.

Louis Claude de Saint-Martin, Philosopher, Mystic

Eventually one grows tired of trying to rearrange external circumstances to suit one's whim. Such an approach leads to exhaustion because some circumstance will always be out of whack with the master plan. Seeking to control one's own mental outlook and self-discipline will be more fruitful, since a well-governed approach to life can deal with any change of circumstance. The person who has learned to control his or her own mind will be more content than the most productive titan of industry. Having a placid, amiable disposition takes a great deal of work, but it is well worth the effort.

This morning, as you begin your day, resolve to work on your inner disposition. Realize that today something will not go according to plan. You will encounter rude people. Accidents will happen. You will make a mistake or one of your associates will. With a great force of mental intention, say to yourself that you will not take the bait. You will not become perturbed when things go wrong. You will allow adverse circumstances to flow around you while working constructively to resolve the problem. You will let go of reactive mental states as soon as they arise.

Feelings of Goodwill

Our life is nothing but the continuity of . . . actions, and they are nothing but the continuity of the whole universe.

Kōun Yamada, Former Leader of Sanbo Kyodan Zen Lineage

Dwelling on the surface of things, we often have the impression of an interminable sequence of mundane trivialities. Most people do many of the same things each day: going to the same job, living in the same house, eating the same food, and so forth. For the ordinary consciousness, this will eventually instill a torturous boredom. For the mindful person, though, a space opens in which each occasion opens onto the infinite, and all the worlds are contained in each interaction. This sounds fantastic and romantic, but the vision of the whole can be obtained by the average person with a modicum of effort in a few days' time. To maintain this vision, however, takes great discipline and decades, if not lifetimes, of effort.

This morning, as you breathe deeply for a few minutes of quiet, open your heart and mind to the wonder and possibility that surround you. Leave room for the new and unexpected, for the sense that you could be surprised today by seeing the familiar in a fresh way. Think about all of the myriad factors that go into making each object that you use, each situation in which you find yourself. When the feeling of tedium comes, try to shift your perspective to one of joyful expectation.

Increasing Awareness, Not Productivity

Wealth is excessive when it reduces man [sic] to a middleman and a jobber, when it prevents him, in his preoccupation with material things, from making his spirit the measure of them.

George Santayana, Philosopher

Haste and worry make life into perpetual tedium, a mere accumulation of tasks to be done. The greatest failing of contemporary society has been its tendency to reduce life to productivity, to make all things measurable and subject to optimization. The qualitative life of poetry and religion, of dance and music, gets lost in the desire to track units of production. Social media and portable technologies have us tracking ourselves: our whereabouts each moment of the day, intake of calories and output of exercise, the happenstance of daily life and our media diets. In all of this tracking and measuring, we forget to be aware of the present moment, to tune into its deeper beauty and significance.

Mindfulness practice brings about a radical simplification and causes life to revolve around a different axis. Resolve to yourself: *I will begin to come back to this present moment, to increase my awareness rather than my productivity. I will begin to turn away from distraction rather than seeking it out. I will stop mentally racing ahead to the future and will stop dwelling in the past.* This morning, cultivate the courage of mind and heart to remain here in this moment. Be a silent witness to everything that arises for you in this moment. When the tendency to pull away presents itself, resist it for as long as possible. Allow the rest of your day to pass without comment, without agitation, without desire or regret.

Countering Skeptical Doubts

When we get stuck in a certain place, it's a place where history will not repeat herself, and that's what makes it even more exciting! . . . The method and the trick and the way it's gonna look are going to be very different than what we've seen before, because we've used all the methods from before. . . . It all has to do with curiosity: what makes something do something?

Richard Feynman, Physicist

Do not ask yourself how the experts do it, how the spiritual masters go about practicing mindfulness. Instead, ask how to make it work for you, in your life and circumstances. All of the advice in the world will not work if it cannot be assimilated into your own place and time, if it cannot be brought into your life story and your worldview. You can read and study the Vedas and the Upanishads, but if you cannot bring them into your life, these venerable texts do you no good. So you must read, study, and, most importantly, apply what you have read. Experiment in your own life with the teachings that have been passed down to you: That is where the real advances can be made.

As you go further in your mindfulness practice, as you persevere and expand your range of practice, wonderful experiences will open to you. This happens as you begin to let go of your reservations and move wholeheartedly into the practice. This morning, you may find yourself slipping back into old ways of thinking, perhaps saying to yourself that you are too busy to practice mindfulness or that it would never work anyway. Counter this skeptical voice with the positive experiences that you have had so far on your journey. Think of the ways that mindfulness practice has already improved your life, and allow that to be your inspiration throughout the day.

Stopping Self-Torture

Seek the unknown way, for the known way is an impasse.

Heraclitus, Ancient Greek Philosopher

If you cannot sit quietly and be contented within yourself, no amount of searching in the world will ever be any comfort. If you cannot delve into the space of a few minutes of silence and emerge with some new point of view on the world, you will be condemned to live in derivative belief systems borrowed from others. Silence restores our relationship with ourselves, and, in this way, it also becomes curative for our relationships with others. From this one still point, this center, all other interactions take their character. If I am impatient with myself, I will also be impatient with others. If I am angry with myself, I will also be angry with others. And yet, who is this *I*? It is a series of interactions that can be either harsh or peaceful, either frantic or calm. So we can choose the tenor of our lives from the quality of our mental states.

Practice being gentle with yourself this morning. Can you give yourself the same unconditional love that the great religions of the world recommend as a way to treat others? This may feel odd at first, but try it anyway. You should begin to feel a relaxing, a loosening inside like you have more room to breathe. As you go easier on yourself, you will also begin to have more patience for others.

Look Around This Room

Those who see all creatures in themselves and themselves in all creatures know no fear. Those who see all creatures in themselves and themselves in all creatures know no grief. How can the multiplicity of life delude the one who sees its unity?

Isha Upanishad, Trans. Eknath Easwaran

We know about observation as a method of science, and we may think about observation as it applies to Sherlock Holmes mystery novels. But what if we took the techniques of Sir Arthur Conan Doyle's Baker Street detective and applied them to our own lives? What if we noticed the trivialities of everyday life and inquired into the motivations behind them? What if we said, "I am avoiding Joe. I wonder why I am doing that." What if we said, "I feel horrible when I wear this ugly brown sweater. Why do I keep doing that?" Then if we keep the inquiry going, we might see into the habits of the past that have made us who we are today. In addition, we see how each and every thing is connected to everything else, that we all share a common destiny.

This morning, imagine for a second that a complete stranger is seeing you for the first time. What would this person think of you? What adjectives would this person use to describe you? Would this description accord with how you see yourself? Is there perhaps some distortion in your self-image that does not match with the reality on the ground? Is there something you can do to make your life match your ideals a little better? Simply notice what needs to be changed. Spend a few minutes on this exercise and then go about your day.

Breathe In the Light

Depression may be rampant around us, but it is impossible to feel depressed at the same time that one feels grateful. Moods come and go, and we may have little emotional or chemical control over them, but feeling and expressing gratitude are choices, and they can punctuate and temper dark emotional states.

Carolyn Baker, Psychotherapist

When you find yourself trapped in a negative emotional state, begin with deep breathing. This inserts a pause between the reactive state and the desired state. As you breathe deeply, pay attention to the breath and let go of the internal dialogue, which acts as a reinforcement mechanism for the negative emotions. Then cultivate in your mind and heart a more positive state, the desired thought or feeling: You could think about peace, love, or gratitude. Perhaps you could think of a time when you felt that way and bring it to mind again, or use an image from your spiritual tradition.

This morning, as you greet the rising sun, picture a bright light at the base of your spine. Recognize that this light represents infinite love, perfection, and goodness. With each new inhalation, draw the light a little farther up the spinal column, to the genitals, the solar plexus, the heart, the throat, between the eyes, and finally to the crown of the head. Make the light more intense as you go, and build the feeling of pure love and perfection as much as possible.

Lengthen Your Interior Silence

The best way to tame vexations is to prevent them from arising and becoming strong. Once they arise, they are best tamed by vigorous practice.

Ch'an Master Sheng-yen

Beautiful moments of clarity and illumination arise by themselves, but you must first give them room to breathe. This can be done through regular mindfulness practice. Mindfulness practice, while undertaking daily affairs, has its root in the morning practice of silent listening. Even if you belong to a tradition that involves studying or chanting scripture, make sure to include some intervals of silence. This allows the mantras or prayers to have some room to work. If you practice regularly every morning, your daily life will begin to be transformed.

Today, try extending your morning meditation. See if you can sit in silent listening for twenty minutes. If that doesn't feel like a stretch to you, try half an hour or an hour. Cultivate the interior silence and see if you can take that silence with you as you continue your daily activities. Blend intense effort with spontaneity. You will notice some effects immediately, while other effects may take a few days to arise. If you can, lessen your duties for a few days and seek some solitude. Reduce entertaining distractions.

Use Your Discomfort As a Guide

Nothing rests; everything moves; everything vibrates.

The Kybalion, *Early Twentieth-Century Hermetic Text by the Three Initiates*

We want certainty in a world of confusion, stability in a world of flux, finality in a world of change. We cannot stop this continual process of upheaval and renewal that characterizes existence: We can only participate in the processes that we find to be the most rewarding and beneficial. What goes by the name of *tradition* is really a flowing stream, a transmission from one generation to the next. The disciple who takes refuge in the guru (literally, *remover of darkness*) or teacher assumes the processes and practices that the previous generations have found to be helpful and beneficial. In this way, the spiritual seeker does not have to start from the beginning but can join midstream.

This morning, look at the areas in your life where you have a discomfort with change. This discomfort signals some hidden attachment. Once you see that you have an attachment, look at it as closely as possible. This can be done without judgment: Just observe the dynamics at work. Feel in your heart center a willingness to let go of the object of attachment. Let that willingness expand as much as possible. Remember that *letting go* does not have to mean stoicism or a lack of care and concern: It just means that you release your obsessive frame of mind.

Smooth the Rough Edges

The man who is kind and practices righteousness, who remains passive amidst the affairs of the world, who considers all creatures on earth as his own self, He attains the Immortal Being, the true God is ever with him.

Kabir, Indian Mystic Poet, Saint

We cannot all go and live in forest huts, and we cannot all practice great religious austerities. It would be wrong to put aside our duties for the sake of a romantic ideal of enlightenment. Our own duties, well performed, will benefit us more than trying to achieve a heroic ideal of the spiritual person. But that does not mean that, even though we are ordinary people, we should not try to reach enlightenment. We should let the daily concerns of life become the grinding stones that make grains of wheat into flour. We should perform those disciplines that we can perform, in our own way, in our own time and place. In this way, we create a more compassionate society, a more peaceful home life, and a more contented inner life.

As you sit for a few minutes this morning, think about the rough edges of your own personality. Perhaps you do not do anything criminal, but do you utter unkind words? Do you engage in gossip and criticism? Search your personality for those places where you lack discipline and resolve to restrain yourself the next time tempting situations arise. Be mindful of the inner conversation, be mindful of the other person, and be mindful of animals and the planet. Resolve to live in the world as a person who has no enemies, as a person who cannot be harmed, as one who wills the good of all.

Truly See and Hear

Ascend with the greatest sagacity from earth to heaven, and unite together things inferior and superior; thus you will possess the light of the whole world, and all obscurity will fly away from you.

The Emerald Tablet of Hermes Trismegistus, Hermetic Text, Trans. Blavatsky

The eyes do not see all that is to be seen, and the ears do not hear all that is to be heard. The mind filters the report of the senses; therefore, a narrowly directed mind will perceive a narrow slice of reality. The person who wishes to see and hear must first undertake the inner alchemy of fighting against all craving, fighting against all presuppositions. The seeker must abandon everything known and plunge into the unknown, making friends with uncertainty and pressing into it as far as possible. Otherwise, the new day being born will be missed, reduced to another iteration of the known.

This morning, as you greet the day, resolve to let go of all that you know about the world. Endeavor to see things in a fresh light like a young child. Forget your past habits and inclinations, and make a silent vow to abide by any insights you receive, no matter how small. Resolve to follow intuition, or the spirit, wherever it leads, even if it means abandoning your old way of life. Further promise to follow the path of mindfulness all the days of your life, awakening to each new insight as it arises.

Try Not to "Fix" the World

When you get out of the driver's seat, you find that life can drive itself, that actually life has always been driving itself. . . . Life becomes almost magical. The illusion of the "me" is no longer in the way. Life begins to flow, and you never know where it will take you.

Adyashanti, Author, Spiritual Teacher

Needing to be in control lies at the root of much suffering and conflict. When we try to *fix* the world in the direction that most suits us, we feel like a failure if things do not change. This leads to self-blame, which, in turn, leads to self-harm. But if we never have the illusion that we control reality, we can go along with events as they arise, sensing the appropriate direction in the moment, but not manipulating and twisting events into a master plan. Everything happens spontaneously, and we don't have to use reserves of energy on frustration and anger.

After a few minutes of deep breathing, ask yourself what you have a strong need to control. See if you can let go, at least a little bit, and let that part of your life take care of itself. This may feel a little irresponsible at first, but persevere in the practice. As you go through the day, awaken to the peace that comes when you let go of the need to control, and make decisions spontaneously. Perhaps you will see that you were never in control in the first place.

When you get out
of the driver's seat,
you find that life can drive itself,
that actually life has
always been driving itself. . . .

Life becomes almost magical.

The illusion of the "me" is no longer
in the way. Life begins to flow,
and you never know
where it will take you.

—ADYASHANTI,
AUTHOR,
SPIRITUAL TEACHER

Connection and Thanksgiving

The simpler and more obvious the discovery, the less equipped we are to figure it out by complicated methods.

Nassim Taleb, Philosopher, Mathematician, Risk Analyst

On some level, we are told that human beings are social animals, but we tend to put a pretty big firewall between biology and politics or ethics. If we can once more recall the *social* in *social animal*, we will feel much less at a loss for contentment, for belonging, for love. The awakened mind has learned once more that it does not belong to itself but exists through and for others, that the social is the ground and precondition for life.

This morning, as you rise to greet the new day, think for a minute of all of the teachers and mentors you have had in life, of your parents and friends. Think of the wild places where you played as a child. Think of the natural systems that give you food, water, and shelter. Cultivate a sense of gratitude for this *beyond self* that made you and sustains you. Realize that you emerge out of a vast array of extra-human conditions, that you would not exist without these intricate systems that go far beyond you, beyond human society to nature itself.

Everything Falling Into Place

There is nothing either good or bad, but thinking makes it so.

Hamlet, *William Shakespeare*

Westerners have become accustomed to thinking of time as an arrow, moving always forward in a linear fashion. We think of ourselves as perched on the razor's edge between a never-arriving future and an always-gone past. This concept of time would be foreign to most of the people for whom ancestors are every bit as *present* as those alive today. In Asian societies and many indigenous traditions, time is cyclical in nature, not linear, as the patterns repeat over generations. The person close to you in this lifetime might have been close to you for many previous lifetimes.

The *arrow of time* concept, which goes back to the ancient Greek philosopher Zeno of Elea, causes much anxiety, since everything must, by definition, be done now or not at all. But what if you were to shift your thinking to believe that everything is already implicitly done? What if you believed that you were living in a present that is already past, already accomplished? Sometimes such a belief is criticized as fatalistic, but it also produces a good deal of freedom. As you set about your morning, picture everything already accomplished, from your first deep breath of the morning to closing your eyes at night. Picture everything falling into place, as it was always meant to be, as it has already been written.

Think of Life As Improvisation

For everything there is a season, and a time for every purpose under heaven.

Ecclesiastes 3:1

Living is one vast musical improvisation, and trouble results from being out of touch with the other players. When we cling too rigidly to what we want to have happen, to our own idea of the unfolding piece, it produces a lack of harmony with the whole. At the same time, if we have no idea of what we want, we can easily get lost and not express our own talents. So there must be a give and take, a melody and a harmony, a back-and-forth between others and ourselves. Sometimes we have a pause or a rest, sometimes the melody, sometimes a solo. We must not think that we have to do everything or that what we do does not matter.

As you center yourself this morning, let go of preconceived notions of what your day will be like. Hold your thoughts in suspension, and be prepared for anything, *good* or *bad*. Think of the qualities that you would like to bring forward in your interactions with others. It will also be okay to think of one or two *action items*, but not a whole litany of unrealistic expectations. Inhale and exhale deeply, and, as you cross over the threshold of your home or office, inhale peace and relaxation as you go about your business.

The Heart As the Hearth of the Body

The longer each of us lives, the greater the likelihood that we will absorb atoms that were once part of Joan of Arc and Jesus Christ, of Neanderthal people and woolly mammoths. As we have breathed in our forebears, so our grandchildren and their grandchildren will take us in with their breath. . . . Every breath is a sacrament, an affirmation of our connection with all other living things.

David T. Suzuki, Zoologist, Environmental Activist

The firebird is a central figure in Russian folklore, musically rendered in Stravinsky's *Firebird Suite*. The firebird's brilliant plumage lights the night and grants hope for the hero's journey. We sometimes forget that each moment has the magic of the firebird—that each breath, each moment, holds the chance to begin anew, to turn away from destructive patterns and toward more holistic patterns of life and thought. Each time we breathe deeply, we resurrect the firebird and allow its colorful plumes to dance through our halls. Each time we catch ourselves and pull back from anger and resentment, we allow the firebird to resume its dance.

The heart center is the hearth of the body, the center of life and warmth. As you breathe deeply this morning, using more and more capacity in your lungs, you will begin to feel greater physical warmth coming into your body. This is the life force called prana, chi, or spirit. Feel that warmth moving into your heart, and grow the inner fire as brightly as possible. Just as a blacksmith uses a bellows to make the fire grow white-hot, allow your lungs to be the bellows of your heart and spirit. If any negative or doubtful thoughts should enter into your consciousness, burn them in the refining fire. Carry this blazing heart center with you throughout your day.

Trade Cynicism for Enthusiasm

When movement of thought stops, sometimes another power descends or arises to spontaneously guide the treatment. Love is the word we usually associate with this divine force which, uncalled for, arises to replace the healer, the healed, and the healing. . . . This Love is not possible to know, to understand, or to grasp. It is the true healing force, for it is the very source itself.

Atreya, Ayurvedic Healer

Cynicism in our time masquerades as realism, as direct access to the truth. The psychic armor of cynicism purports to offer an unvarnished view of the world as it is while actually filtering and manipulating the truth. Cynicism, as a worldview, is easy to adopt but difficult to put down. It is easy to adopt because it asks us to invest little in the way of time and energy. It is hard to put down because it creates a cozy hollow place where nothing can ever affect us. Cynicism eventually produces a deadening effect on the emotions and a constricting impact on our ability to act in the world.

This morning, notice your reactions to positive news. Do you instinctively find ways to turn a positive into a negative? Suppose a new cancer treatment has been found by a bright young graduate student at a major research institution. Would your first impulse be to say, "Wow! That's wonderful!" or "I bet some pharmaceutical company is going to make billions off of that!" This morning, look at these filters and open yourself to the possibility that there may be more good in the world than you think.

Look for Solutions in Process

To a deva, the garden is not an assembly of various forms and colors but rather moving lines of energy. . . . Within this field of energy, each plant was an individual whirlpool of activity.

The Findhorn Foundation, a Spiritual Community

What looks to our eyes like an object, a thing in stasis, is actually a process or nested series of processes. I am reminded of a particular marble staircase at my undergraduate institution. So many people had gone up and down the steps over the decades that the steps had a sag in the middle where the stone had worn away. To compensate for this dip in the middle, metal treads had to be installed to prevent falls. What looks stable is actually undergoing constant change. The marble itself is a process, formed over millions of years of geologic time. The steps are a process, and the metal treads are a process. This is true whether we are looking at biological organisms or inanimate *things.* Nothing remains untouched: Everything interacts with everything else, up close and at a distance.

This morning, what do you assume are the *givens* of your life? What do you think cannot change? What has proven to resist the most stubborn acts of willfulness? Now break that seeming stability down into the subprocesses that give rise to it. See how far you can go in breaking down each problem and situation into its constituent parts. Once you have gone as far as you can go, sit and meditate silently for a few minutes. Then go about your daily life. Later in the day, you will be surprised to find that a new line of inquiry or a solution will appear out of nowhere.

Waiting with Mindfulness

For much of life, things happen when they happen. The bus arrives when it arrives. . . . Our soup is warm when it's warm. . . . We can generally do things to influence this process, like take a different bus route . . . or buy a more powerful microwave, but . . . we're still waiting—waiting while wishing for some other experience.

Jonathan Kaplan, Psychologist

Our lives are bookended by birth and death, punctuated with smaller milestones in between. In fact, we are always in between one event and another. We wait for the weekend, wait for vacation, wait for retirement, wait for the release of a new book or movie. Waiting can be unpleasant and angst producing, or pleasant and euphoric, depending upon the attitude taken toward it. Think about the comparison between waiting in line at the Department of Motor Vehicles and waiting for a loved one to return from a long journey. We can actually take downtime of any sort and turn it into a power of tuning in to the present moment. We can test ourselves by refusing to get bent out of shape and, instead, entering into a space of acceptance and peace.

What are you waiting for this morning? Are you waiting for a package, a phone call, a promotion? For a few minutes, lean into the sometimes unpleasant in-between feeling. Observe its contours more closely, including its effects on your mind and body. Breathe into that emotional state, whether it is excited, anxious, or ambiguous. See if you can live here in this space of tension between having and not having. Notice the many in-betweens throughout the day, and notice that life is lived on the threshold, always arriving.

Release Tension

When all desires that surge in the heart are renounced, the mortal becomes immortal. When all the knots that strangle the heart are loosened, the mortal becomes immortal. This sums up the teaching of the scriptures.

Katha Upanishad, Trans. Eknath Easwaran

Mindfulness, unlike most other pursuits, does not require more of us, but less. Do the normal things—cleaning, exercising, and working—but give your heart to what is called emptiness, the divine, or God. This takes a bit of effort—to still the constant internal noise—but the effort is well worth any difficulty that arises from it. Such a pursuit is not selfish or antisocial because natural love and affection wells in the heart of the one who intentionally practices mindfulness. This warmth will be felt by every person in your life.

This morning, as you rise to the light of a new day, let go of anything that might have you preoccupied, whether that might be a specific worry or a physical pain or ailment. Breathe into the pain and worry, and picture the troublesome knots of problems becoming looser. Allow your thoughts to become light and easy and have the attitude that all trouble will be resolved as you hold gracefully to inner peace.

Don't Get Taken by Your Own Thoughts

One of the hallmarks of experienced meditators is their ability to experience negative emotions without necessarily "getting caught up" in them. This skill has significant implications for the treatment of common forms of psychopathology, particularly mood and anxiety disorders.

Michael Treadway, Neuroscientist, and Sara Lazar, Psychiatrist

A negative feedback loop exists between fraught internal dialogue, physical states of the body (particularly shallow breathing and rapid heart rate), and states of the brain (such as the production of stress hormones). To put it simply, thinking about a problem excessively only magnifies the perception of doom and gloom. The brain and body respond to every perceived threat as though it were a real threat: The body and mind believe what you tell them to believe. To slow down and eventually reverse this cycle, it is necessary to intervene mentally by moving out of a mode of frantic self-talk and into a mode of observation. It is also necessary to intervene physically by slowing down the breath and deepening it, which puts the brakes on the stress response. With much practice, it will then be possible to reintroduce more positive thoughts through practices like mantra and visualization.

This morning, look at any afflictive emotions or thoughts that arise in your mind. Rather than allowing them to railroad you into an interior monologue, simply observe the troubling mental processes. Allow them to wash over you and through you. Think of them like waves at the beach or like a thunderstorm. They do not control you: They simply exist around you. The troubling thoughts are processes of nature with factors that give rise to them and other factors that cause them to evaporate. Seek to understand these factors, and you will be able to escape from the trap laid for you.

Get Out of the Boat and Swim

Most people are deeply attached to thinking. . . . Most people celebrate thought and value their ideas as their most personal property. Thinking is the tool by which they control their own world, both outer and inner. Letting go of thought and entering into mindful silence means dropping the attachment to control of their domain.

Ajahn Brahm, Theravada Buddhist Monk

Most of us have good excuses that explain why we are not doing the practice of mindfulness, or other disciplines like seated meditation or chanting or puja. We have long to-do lists to think about, jobs to perform, families who need us, and so forth. But behind all of these excellent reasons for not doing the practice is the fear that we might have to truly face ourselves in the process. We might have to see those aspects of our personalities that are less than perfect and we may be asked to do something about them. We might be confronted with our addictions and be asked to do without them. So we do not practice or we practice half-heartedly, telling ourselves how sensible we are. Really, we are just afraid.

One of the strongholds of a non-mindful life is thought, that trusty rowboat that has gotten us through so many stormy waters. We like the boat so much that we do not want to go for a swim, even if the waters are warm, azure blue, and filled with coral and fish. We would rather stay safe, thank you, with a life preserver and a heavy anchor. This morning, try to do without thought. It will be a great triumph to manage a few seconds, and then a bit more. Examine whether your thought processes really protect you as much as you think they do, or whether they, at least sometimes, prevent you from fully engaging with life.

Most people are deeply
attached to thinking. . . .

Most people celebrate thought and
value their ideas as their
most personal property.

Thinking is the tool by which they control
their own world, both outer and inner.

Letting go of thought and
entering into mindful silence
means dropping the attachment
to control of their domain.

—AJAHN BRAHM, THERAVADA
BUDDHIST MONK

Do What Makes You Sane and Balanced

As you bend over backward to please others, even people you don't know well, you may get out of touch with your own physical and emotional limits and simply do too much. Your own self-care is likely to suffer as a result of an ongoing external focus combined with pushing yourself beyond your limits.

Micki Fine, Psychologist, Counselor

When we try to be good people, unselfish people, the trouble is that we are always making assumptions about what other people want and then molding our behavior to fit accordingly. But there is always a mismatch between what we think other people want and what they actually want. As a result, when we try to please others, we may end up making them unhappy *and* ourselves unhappy. The phrase *please follow your bliss* has become a cliché, but there is a certain amount of truth to it. We don't need to be pushy or rude, but doing the things that feed our spirits is more likely to produce well-being for all parties concerned than a blind form of self-sacrifice.

You probably have several activities in your life that make you a more calm and balanced person. Maybe you like taking walks in the woods, knitting colorful scarves, or writing short stories. Could you take a few minutes this morning to engage in one of these favorite pursuits? If not, could you make a concrete plan to do so later in the day or later in the week? Examine any fears that you have about doing the things that you love. You may be afraid that someone will be displeased with you or that you won't be able to accomplish your *real* work. Acknowledge these fears, but don't let them stop you from doing the things that make you glad to be alive.

Miracle Addicts Anonymous

May we follow the path that leads to real bliss and where there is no crime; treading on which one is far from all animosity and achieves the wealth supreme.

Yajur Veda IV.29

Meditating won't make all your problems go away immediately. All sorts of claims are made for meditation: that you can learn to levitate, appear in two places at once, emit a floral scent, etc. Maybe such things do, in fact, happen, but should they become the focus and ultimate goal? I sometimes wonder if the supernatural focus does more harm than good, because the person who has just gotten started will be discouraged when no miracles are forthcoming. By contrast, expecting something more modest—like a light and buoyant, joyful feeling in the heart—will be more realistic and encouraging. Meditation largely solves problems by stripping life down to its bare essentials, not by adding miraculous powers. If amazing feats and experiences (what are called *siddhis*, perfections or powers) come, then great, but don't make them the litmus test for whether or not your practice is working. In fact, abandon all thoughts of whether or not the practice is *working*, as this is a form of destructive doubt.

Have you been curious about the supernatural or paranormal in the past? Do you crave stories of wonderworking and the paranormal? You might have noticed how such cravings trivialize *normal,* everyday experiences. This morning, rather than reaching out for the fantastic and the larger-than-life, seek to see the beauty and joy in everyday life. Recover a sense of wonder with the here and now. Then your faith and perseverance will become unshakable. You will be able to enter into the most mundane of situations with your tranquility intact.

Mindfulness As Medicine

*The empirical literature suggests that mindfulness meditation and
the MBSR [mindfulness-based stress reduction] program may lead
to reduced symptoms in a variety of problematic medical conditions
and illnesses, including chronic pain, stress-related disorders, anxiety,
depression, binge eating, fibromyalgia, and psoriasis, as well as ancillary
symptoms associated with some forms of cancer and multiple sclerosis.*

Joshua Wootton, Psychologist in Pain Management

We have this medicine called meditation or mindfulness readily available to us, now proven through decades of scientific research. It costs nothing, and the basic technique can be learned in half an hour. So why don't we use it more often? It seems we have a bias toward complexity, that, if something is complicated, it must be better. We also have a bias in medicine against preventative treatments and toward costly, after-the-fact interventions. Our society seems intent on learning things the hard way, and this can be seen in many arenas of life. We would rather wait and see how bad a problem will become than address it head-on.

This morning, you owe it to your future self, to your loved ones, and to your world not to let your stressful life become overwhelming. As you breathe deeply and let go of the past and future, say to yourself, "Whatever happens today, I will remain within my calm center. If something happens to take me away from my calm center, I can return to it at any time." Continue with the deep breathing, and, if disruptive thoughts occur, say to yourself again, "Whatever happens today, I will remain within my calm center . . . ." Let the *medicine* of mindfulness work on your body.

Build a Bridge to Your Dreams

All the great Teachers have laid stress upon the importance, not of envisaging an enormous period of time before you to do the difficult things of the spiritual life, but to pay attention to the little passing moments, the minutes and hours of each day. Therefore they taught: Fill the day full; watch over it, guide it; regard each single day as if it were the last day that you knew you were going to live.

A. Trevor Barker, Theosophist

Imagine a great chasm like a gorge or canyon with a decrepit bridge going across, missing several wooden slats. It would take a great deal of courage to cross that bridge. If the chasm represents crossing over to some great life goal, each day would be one wooden slat on that bridge. The more days that you miss in working toward that goal, the more the bridge falls into disrepair. The more days that you practice, the more trustworthy and sturdy the bridge becomes. In the spiritual life, each day of work is another day that the bridge from here to there will remain in good repair, will be a sure way to cross over the chasm.

This morning you may be thinking of your life's quest, the reason you get out of bed each day. Your quest may be something quite large, something so big that it is intimidating to think about. But if you think of doing only one day's work, suddenly this impossible task is brought down to scale.

Think for a few minutes about what you need to do today to make your dream a reality. Build your bridge one wooden slat at a time. If you do that one thing, you can live this day with purpose and conviction. Each time you feel discouraged, come back to one simple task that you can achieve in short order.

Encouraging the Culture of Mindfulness

Enlightenment for everyone? It sounds like too grandiose a Utopia, especially when we consider how inept human beings seem in the face of the harsh realities which confront the planet today. . . . Yet the human species has long shown a . . . surprising aptitude for improving itself. The process is called cultural evolution. It continues currently to civilize billions of humans along many positive, fruitful lines.

James H. Austin, Neurologist

Mindfulness does promote relaxation, but the practice can become far more than that when practiced by enough people over a long period of time. The dispositions to act in positive ways engendered by mindfulness practice then lead to tangible actions to transform society for the better. As more people come to crave a more harmonious way of life, they support one another in efforts to live purposefully and mindfully. At this point, a critical mass develops that can transform educational institutes, places of business, and our home lives in ways that protect and foster the spiritual life. This emerging society will have loving kindness as a basic value and yet will also incorporate the best insights of science and culture.

Perhaps since you have begun your practice, you have started to see a culture of mindfulness emerging. Maybe you have a friend who meditates or maybe you pass a Hindu temple on the way to work. Try to make one connection to make your practice more sustainable over the long term. Enroll in a class, pick up a book, or create a space in your home to take your practice to the next level. When you are ready, make a promise to keep doing your mindfulness practice every day, for as long as it takes, until it becomes a reflexive part of your personality.

No Castigation,
No Congratulation

Sometimes we stop using skills because we are feeling better. At other times, old thinking and behaviors return despite our best efforts, and we begin to experience more frequent, severe, longer-lasting, and disruptive negative moods. As bad as this feels, it can be an opportunity to further develop our skills and help them become more automatic.

Dennis Greenberger and Christine Padesky, Psychologists

The minute-to-minute thoughts that recur in our heads become part of the emotional wallpaper of our lives. Our thoughts and emotions are tightly coupled: What affects thought affects emotion and vice versa. So we have to transform them together. This takes a lot of persistence over a long period of time, and it involves doing both inner and outer work.

As you sit and breathe deeply this morning, note your mood. Perhaps you are feeling irritable or tired, bored or restless, excited or nervous. Just see what is there within you: Do not feel the need to castigate yourself if you are not feeling chipper or congratulate yourself if you are feeling well. Notice that this state in which you find yourself is temporary and subject to change. As you begin to observe it, you may see it changing already. Do not seek to deliberately control your thoughts and emotions: Just let them come and go. The act of awareness alone has transformative power.

Name the
Awe-Inspiring Presence

Awakened now, I shall not allow myself to be victimized by Maya (illusion). . . . I am now a bee at my Lord's Lotus Feet and shall not allow my mind to leave the nectar of their enjoyment for a moment.

Goswami Tulsidas, Hindu Poet and Saint

The world holds snare after snare for the mind that loses its vigilance. These snares are not just the oft-warned-against cravings for food and sex. Anything that engrosses the mind, anything that produces obsession, leads away from the path of liberation. Mantra (literally, that which takes away the mind) cuts these bonds as soon as they are formed, and, for this reason, the various world traditions have recommended repeating the names of God. By substituting the thought of the divine for the distracted thought, the devotee is able to cut loose from desire.

This morning, try repeating a name for God from your own religious tradition. Repetition can be counted on a mala (rosary), or the name can be chanted for a predetermined period of time. If you don't have a religious tradition, it is okay to experiment with a mantra or prayer that attracts you. Otherwise, try a word like *peace* or *joy*. Keep yourself going in the practice until it becomes almost automatic. Then you can repeat the name no matter what you might be doing at the time.

Managing Anger

Anger can be a master illusionist. Angry, hostile, or scornful feelings can fool you into believing that you are permanently and unalterably isolated from other human beings or any life around you.

Jeffrey Brantley, Psychiatrist

For those of us who were raised in religious households or homes with an excess of politeness, it can be extremely uncomfortable to express anger or even admit that you have it. We can develop a taboo around anger that makes it nearly impossible to address directly. The first step in working with anger is to realize that simply having feelings of anger does not make you a bad person. Anger, just like any other emotion, is a temporary state arising from conditions around you and the patterns of your mental make-up. Observing anger and the thoughts that go along with it can create a little bit of wiggle room in which you can begin to generate a new pattern.

What situations in your life trigger your anger response? Without launching into an internal diatribe, look at the circumstances and persons involved. Are there concrete actions, however small, that you could take to remedy the situation? Are there mindfulness strategies that you can employ the next time anger arises? You may be feeling anger right now as a result of this exercise. Breathe into the feeling of anger and release it. Avoid the reactive thoughts that feed anger. Relax the facial muscles (perhaps a frown or a furrowed brow) that give physical expression to anger. Acknowledge the anger and even welcome it, but do not do anything to continue it. You will see it disappearing as you persist in the practice.

Harness Your Natural Power

Those who forget their own nature, their Godly essence, forget the power within themselves. Our real nature most often is mistaken by others. They prefer to believe in a miracle of the supernatural, rather than the inner strength of the powers that all of us possess.

Sri Trailinga Swami, Hindu Saint

Drops of water, accumulating over time, carve the bed of a spring, then a stream, then a riverbed, then a vast canyon. Nature seems so benign and is yet so powerful. When we observe and understand nature, that same force resides within us. We should never doubt how much we can accomplish, if only we can awaken to that potential and exercise it daily. The plan that is executed a little bit at a time, day by day, will have infinitely greater realization than the plan that, though grandiose, has not been given sufficient time and attention.

Today is a day like any other, and yet it holds immense power. Think this morning about what you would like to achieve, something that taps into your life's purpose, that inspires and delights you. Make a vow this morning to work on that plan of yours every day for as long as it takes. Dedicate your project to the good of all beings and ask for divine blessings. Then get started, if only for a few minutes.

Retiring the Sad Stories
We Tell Ourselves

Mindfulness is awareness that arises through paying attention, on purpose, in the present moment, non-judgementally. It's about knowing what is on your mind.

Jon Kabat-Zinn, Founder of Mindfulness-Based Stress Reduction (MBSR)

We often believe our own sad stories about our lives, and we do so quite unconsciously. In this way, we cast ourselves as victims in our own dramas rather than claiming our power, and with it, our responsibility. We cannot claim responsibility for our own narratives until we first recognize them, together with the conditions and circumstances that give rise to them. Mindfulness practice can be tremendously useful in coming to the awareness of the thought patterns that keep us living in degraded circumstances rather than claiming power and responsibility.

This morning, look within yourself and see if you see traces of a sad, victim story that frequently invades your thought patterns. Who do you blame for the problems in your life? Is it a spouse or partner? Your employer? Yourself? Know that placing blame is an unproductive activity that does not improve the situation. Let go of the blame narrative, or at least loosen it around the edges. Keep a space open there, and invite other possibilities into your life. Come back to this exercise any time the invasive thought pattern comes to mind.

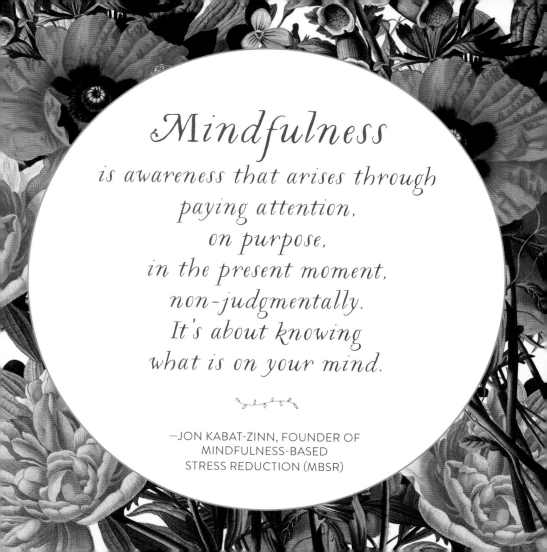

Mindfulness
is awareness that arises through
paying attention,
on purpose,
in the present moment,
non-judgmentally.
It's about knowing
what is on your mind.

—JON KABAT-ZINN, FOUNDER OF
MINDFULNESS-BASED
STRESS REDUCTION (MBSR)

Transcending Limitations

*One who meditates upon and realizes the Self discovers that
everything in the cosmos—energy and space, fire and water, name and
form, birth and death, mind and will, word and deed, mantram and
meditation—all come from the Self.*

Chandogya Upanishad 26.1

Life can often seem slow, dull, boring. It is only at the peak moments that we realize how fleeting it all can be. We have this short time on Earth to live, this brief moment of life. Should we spend it in causing division, in stealing from others, in creating ever more strife? Such actions seem like a waste of a lifetime. And if they are a waste of a lifetime, they are a waste of an hour, a minute, a second. We should instead resolve to bring about something beautiful in the world, something that will inspire others, something that will outlive our own mortal bodies.

There is a difference between wanting *name and fame* for the sake of the ego and wanting to transcend time and place for the benefit of the world. We should seek to transcend those limitations that keep us from being good at serving others. What causes you to hold back in expressing your talents? What causes you to shrink from your divine mission? Take one limitation and reflect on it for a few minutes. Notice its contours. See if you can find a chink in the armor of this seemingly insurmountable obstacle. Take one small action toward expressing your innate divinity.

Bringing Light

Lead me from untruth to truth. Lead me from darkness to light.
Lead me from death to immortality. Om, peace, peace, peace.

Brhadaranyaka Upanishad I.iii.28

We spend most of our lives in a great mental tangle, wondering about our life's purpose and yet also castigating ourselves for not achieving an ill-defined goal. We feel sorry for ourselves for every little slight ever visited upon us, and yet never stop to make amends for the wrongs that we have committed against others. Our bodies fall apart not only from their material, transitory nature, but also because we do not care for them properly through good diet and exercise. Our relationships suffer because of neuroses that have not been properly addressed.

And yet, no matter how far this confused state has continued, there is always time to begin again. We can breathe deeply, let go of anguish, and invite the divine light to dwell within. We can cultivate that light until we become a light for others. We can become ambassadors for peace and justice in the world. This morning, take a few moments to untangle any turbulent thoughts. Breathe in the essence of divine light. Allow it to suffuse your being so that you share light with those you meet today.

Dealing with Difficult People

My habitual desire to control, I now abandon. / And from my schemes so carefully conceived, I release everyone. / And in humility, set you free from me. / My playing God is over. / Now I surrender, surrender, surrender.

Gaura Vani, Kirtan Artist

The trouble with trying to control others is that they do not live up to the fantasy images that we may have of them. Other people were not born to serve us, to cater to our whims, to fix whatever is wrong with us. Instead, we have to encounter them as they are. When we encounter difficult people, grouchy people, mean people, we must first realize that these same tendencies exist within ourselves. Next, we have to find that place where we can work with these people and try to help them to grow without trying to control them.

You may be thinking of someone in your life right now who irritates you beyond belief. This person monopolizes your time and energy. This person talks about you behind your back or hides insults in faint praise. This person never has a kind or encouraging word. Realize that anger will never make this person change. Perhaps this person has been put in your path in order to make you more patient, more humble, more loving. Perhaps this person has been put into your life to make you reach out for support and guidance. Take a few minutes to see how you can deal with difficult people without resorting to controlling behavior and angry outbursts.

Reuniting Scattered Consciousness

At times almost all of us envy the animals. They suffer and die, but they do not seem to make a "problem" of it. Their lives seem to have so few complications. They eat when they are hungry and sleep when they are tired. . . . For the animal, happiness consists in enjoying life in the immediate present—not in the assurance that there is a whole future of joys ahead of him.

Alan Watts, Philosopher

This present moment has a richness and fullness—not only multiple branching futures converging with this hour, but also a depth and texture of its own. When our senses and our mental processes coincide completely, when the mind no longer races ahead into the future or backward into the past, then alone can we see clearly. We come to true acceptance of mistakes made and own up to the present, no longer seeking to avoid it or escape from it. We simply have the life that we have.

As you rise to greet the morning sun, look deeply into this moment. This moment is like the trunk of a tree with many branches. You hold all of the possibilities for the future right here with you. Clue into the qualities and capacities that you would like to develop, and not necessarily the *wish list* for what you would like to have happen. In this way, you *prune* the tree of branching possibilities to the branches that most align with your values.

Stop Forcing Things

Meekness is the absolute courage which does not want to force and cannot force, by virtue of a person's inner state. . . . It is with meekness that the victory must be gained.

Jan van Rijckenborgh, Rosicrucian Teacher

Our movies are filled with action heroes who solve problems by chasing *bad guys* down the street and shooting at them. Our politicians promise swift but questionable action against immigrants, terrorists, or the enemy du jour. Our schools are run by simple metrics of *failing* or *improving*, as though education could be measured so easily. We like toughness; we like simplicity; we like to know where things stand. But the world is infinitely more complicated than any simple measure of right and wrong, and the aggressive path usually creates more problems than it solves. It is much more difficult to actually sort through the moral and social tangles and to take the gentle path that leads to real growth and change.

Our societies equate pacifism with weakness, gentleness with lack of resolve, and yet nothing could be further from the truth. This morning, think of some way in which you might be aggressively forcing a solution that just isn't working. What would it look like to take a step back, to let go? Wait and listen for a few minutes and see if a simpler way appears. Sometimes the courageous way demands doing nothing, or acting in more subtle ways, behind the scenes.

Work with Heart;
Let Go of Reward

We are each a piece of something connected and complicated, something with such constant presence that it is invisible: the network of love and imagination that is the true fabric of humanity. . . . No one does anything alone. Even the greatest inventors build on the work of thousands. Creation is contribution.

Kevin Ashton, Tech Innovator

If we seek to *make our mark* upon the world, we will set ourselves up for failure, for such things can always only be measured after the fact in distorted and hagiographic fashion. Even if we are among the lucky few to achieve acclaim during our lifetimes, the praise may ring hollow, the rewards may feel meaningless. It would be much better to do the things we love because we love them and not from any need for rewards. In this way, we shed the burden of having to be brilliant and save the simple joys of the task itself.

As you set about your day, try to pay attention to the task itself. Whether your work is something you naturally enjoy or something you'd rather not be doing, try to pay full attention to it as much as possible. Notice everything around you: the subtle lilt of a customer's accent, the smoothness of typing paper, the sights and sounds of your place of work. Do your work with heart as well as more traditional forms of effort and see if something shifts inside you. See if you can find greater inspiration and joy in what you do.

Follow Your Muse

*Don't forget love; it will bring you all the madness you need /
to unfurl yourself across the universe.*

Mirabai, Hindu Saint

Everything worth doing has already been done. Everything worth saying has already been said. When this mood strikes you, think about what freedom it should give you. If all of the good words and noble deeds have already been accomplished, you are free to simply dance your own dance and sing your own song. You can be unrestrained, you can improvise, you can structure your path as you go along. You can't break the world: It has already seen it all. If you have to surprise someone, surprise yourself by acting with great abandon to realize the crazy vision that invades your dreams.

When you hold back from living your truth, who are you trying to please? Are you really doing it to please others, or are you secretly afraid of the risks involved in wearing your heart on your sleeve? This morning, allow your God, your muse, your angel, to suffuse your whole self. Resolve that today you will follow that muse without holding anything back, even if other people think you are crazy.

Love Your Body

The Nādīs [subtle channels of the body] are . . . the conduits of Prāna
[primal energy]. Through them its solar and lunar currents run. Could we
see them, the body would present the appearance of those maps which
delineate the various ocean currents. They are the paths along which
Prānashakti [goddess energy] goes.

Sir John Woodroffe (Arthur Avalon), Sanskrit Scholar

In the West, we often think of the body along the lines of a machine meta-phor, as a series of interlocking parts whose interaction is purely physical. In tantric thought, and in many indigenous traditions, the body is a conduit for spiritual energies. It is permeable to all sorts of gods and spirits: It has a physical, material side, yes, but it is much more than that. It is our means of access to the subtle worlds. We should respect it not out of vanity or attachment, but because we can use it to make contact with the divine.

Perhaps you have a tortured history with your own body. You may have struggled with an eating disorder or longed to escape from physical exist-ence altogether. This morning, as you inhale deeply, breathe in love and respect for the body. Think of all the good services that it performs for you. Take special note of those places where you may harbor pain and in-vite divine light to permeate those places.

Reading a Transcript of Your Thoughts

When an answer doesn't occur to us right away, we often get uncomfortable with this emptiness. We fill these gaps with thoughts from our memory bank, destroying the mental silence that could have brought us something fresh. As we shed this vexation and learn to be at ease with the unknown, we increase exponentially the likelihood of experiencing an insight.

Charles Kiefer, Innovation Consultant

To have hope in our lives, genuine hope, we must first open the door to it and give it room to stand, and then invite it for tea, and then give it some room to prop up its feet and stay awhile. There is no place for hope where there is no room for anything new. For something new to arrive, we must first become hospitable to the new and different in our lives. There must be room on the shelf for a new book, room in the cupboard for a new ingredient, room in our minds for a new thought. So the first work in cultivating hope is clearing internal and external space: We have to discard what no longer serves us.

If you could print a transcript of every thought you have ever had, what would you see coming up over and over again? Would it make for an interesting read? Would it be depressing, scary, entertaining, or funny? If you could edit that transcript, what would you keep and what would you throw away? Spend a few minutes *editing* your thought process by letting go, at this very moment, of those thought processes that you would like to discard. When they try to worm their way back again, hold open, as strongly as you can, a space of emptiness and hospitality.

You Do Not Face
Your Troubles Alone

In whom is the universe, who is in the universe, who is the universe; in whom is the soul, who is in the soul, who is the soul; knowing that Truth—and therefore the universe—as our Self, alone extinguishes all fear, brings an end to misery, and leads to infinite freedom.

Swami Vivekananda, Hindu Monk

The sense of separation, of individualism, of willfulness, brings a false confidence and a sense of striving that can never be satisfied. Living into the truth of a preexisting union brings true confidence and an end to striving. The world suffers so much because so many people are deprived of their basic unity with divine truth and power. Consciousness of this unity brings peace in the heart and ends the craving for possessions and status. Realizing this unity means a basic security even in the most adverse conditions.

This morning, realize that whatever you might face today, you remain connected to the universe around you. Do not attempt to use your own power to face things alone. Remain receptive to the source at the heart of reality and draw on its enclosing power. Be mindful of this enfolding energy as it courses through your mind, your heart, your senses, and your body. Allow yourself to be a conduit for the divine as it unfolds in your life. All you really need to do is allow the universe to work through you.

Embrace a Living Tradition

The joy of life consists in the exercise of one's energies, continual growth, constant change, the enjoyment of every new experience. To stop means simply to die. The eternal mistake of mankind is to set up an attainable ideal.

Aleister Crowley, Occultist

The truth behind the many religions, philosophies, and creeds is the desirability of spiritual cultivation, of seeking to become ever more perfect, to become more godlike. We really seek to grow, to change, to become more than we are at present. A dead religion or philosophy is one that asks nothing of us, that yields comfort without asking for anything in return. A living tradition demands our best and then some, has us stretching our arms upward toward the sun, reaching ever higher.

This morning, ask yourself if you have become too staid and comfortable in your life, in your career, in your relationships, in your belief system. Awaken to the boundless potential of your life. Let go of all of your past accomplishments and count them as nothing in the luminous present. Allow your mind to receive the blessing of this day, which holds great things in store for you. Welcome this day with great fervor, with great openness and grace.

Find Depth and Duration in the Present Moment

May the heaven and earth be an armour for me; an armour the day; an armour the Sun. May the resplendent Lord and the adorable Lord be an armour for me. May the sustainer (dhātā) put an armour on me.

Atharva-Veda VIII.5.18

When we perceive that things are not going the way that we want them to go, the unreflective, reactive mind says that we should try harder, push harder, be more aggressive. The internal results of this strategy are passion and anger, which bear fruit in nervous disorders. The external results are greater enmity and loss of allies. Such a strategy can succeed, but it succeeds at great cost. When this dynamic moves beyond the individual level, we have the root conditions for hatred and warfare. So we need a better way to deal with adverse conditions that does not have so many negative implications.

We can shield ourselves from adverse events by taking refuge in the present moment. We can thicken that moment by breathing into it and by paying careful attention to it. Suddenly what seemed like a fleeting instant now has depth and duration. The harried frame of mind now becomes a fortress and a place of rest. The insurmountable problems of life now seem like manageable conditions. Take the first few minutes of this day, whether you are sitting still or actively doing something, to thicken the present moment. Feel these first minutes of the day in all of their texture and liveliness. Notice everything around you, and allow the inner dialogue to fade before the day's brilliance.

Aligning with Inner Purpose

No act is performed without a thought at its root either at the time of performance or as leading to it. These thoughts are lodged in that part of man which we have called Manas—the mind, and there remain as subtle but powerful links with magnetic threads that enmesh the solar system, and through which various effects are brought out.

William Quan Judge, Theosophist

The mindfulness practitioner has a tremendous advantage in life that can make her actions more harmonious and effective. The ignorant person considers only the outward aspect of the deed and does not see the roots of action in thinking, feeling, and willing. By getting down to the root of action in the inner disposition, the adept can bring forth the desired state of mind and, with it, states of the material world that conform to it. This revolution from the inside out creates not just favorable mental conditions but a whole life more conducive to peace and goodwill.

You may find yourself reacting to events, always catching up to external reality. This morning, resolve to do things the other way around. For a few minutes, meditate on feelings of peace, contentment, and goodwill. See the circumstances of your life completely aligning with your inner purpose, gradually but unfailingly moving you toward liberation. Close your meditation with gratitude for this transformation that is taking place even now.

Avoid Beating Yourself Up

The more openhearted we are with ourselves, the closer we feel toward the rest of life. Self-compassion is the foundation for kindness toward others.

Christopher K. Germer, Psychologist

Many kind and compassionate people in the world would never kick a dog, but they have no trouble at all beating up on themselves emotionally. Kicking a dog is, of course, a terrible thing to do that solves nothing, not even bad behavior on the part of the dog. In the same way, casting aspersion on ourselves is both ineffective and morally wrong. Our bodies, together with our emotional and mental processes, are the vehicles that we have for navigating our way through the world. We should, therefore, be respectful of ourselves and kind to ourselves. This can be as difficult as the most austere religious observances, but it releases a lot of emotional troubles and helps us to better relate to others.

This morning, you may be castigating yourself for something minor. Perhaps you overslept or forgot a friend's birthday or missed paying a bill. Rather than overreacting through self-blame, think of the good qualities that you have and the other areas of your life that are going well. Fill your heart with feelings of love and confidence, and this will help you improve your connections with others.

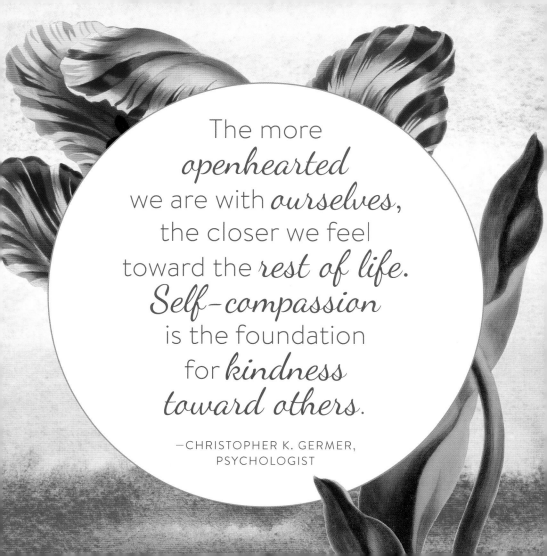

The more *openhearted* we are with *ourselves,* the closer we feel toward the *rest of life.* *Self-compassion* is the foundation for *kindness toward others.*

—CHRISTOPHER K. GERMER,
PSYCHOLOGIST

Taking What Comes

Beyond the beauty of the external forms, there is more here: something that cannot be named, something ineffable, some deep, inner, holy essence. Whenever and wherever there is beauty, this inner essence shines through somehow. It only reveals itself to you when you are present.

Eckhart Tolle, Spiritual Author

If you are one of the lucky ones, one of those with enough perseverance of vision, you have seen the shimmering reality within the many things. This vision may have erupted upon you suddenly, or it may have taken years of disciplined practice to see it. Once you got a glimpse of this *pearl of great price* (Matthew 13:45–46), you would sell all you own to see it again. The vision came, and, as quickly as it appeared, disappeared, not wanting to be bought. It left you there, feeling bereft, but you had to go back to ordinary life and ordinary seeing.

As you look back on your spiritual life, you undoubtedly see many highs and lows—times when you felt complete despair and times when you felt indescribable bliss. The natural response is to crave the highs and hate the lows, but you can't have one without the other. To leave behind the first forays into spirituality, you must take what comes, high or low. This morning, resolve to continue in the practice of mindfulness, whether you feel inspired or depressed, energetic or lethargic, joyful or sad. To be mindful is to attend to all of the states of consciousness as they occur, not to paint everything in sunshine and rainbows and pretend that everything is okay or to wallow in despair and pretend that nothing is good.

Find Guidance in Silence

The voice is identified as Ruah, which is the Old Testament word for the Spirit of God. . . . It has spoken to me sporadically since I was in high school. I expect that if a crisis arises it will say something again. . . . I have to be very receptive to hear it. It sounds as though it's coming from millions of miles away.

Philip K. Dick, Science Fiction Author

In order to get in touch with inspiration, we have to first get really quiet, which is about the most difficult thing to do in our world. When we have sufficiently withdrawn from society and everything gets really still, a very subtle form of guidance asserts itself. Call it the muse, call it an angel, call it a divine sign, call it the gods or God, something speaks there or nudges there. It gives us guidance on how to live, advice about a project, or just keeps us company. This very odd phenomenon is easily missed in our age, and it is inconvenient for materialism.

If you find yourself with a pressing question this morning, like a need for overarching guidance in life, try getting silent for a few days. Try not to read too much or try not to listen to the news. Allow yourself only a few lines of scripture. Do several periods of silent meditation. Then ask your question. If you don't get an answer, do some more periods of silence. If you persevere for as long as it takes, you will find inner guidance that will point you in the right direction.

Unplugging
(At Least Some of the Time)

You don't actually know a time or a culture until you discover the thoughts that its people can't allow themselves to think.

John Michael Greer, Archdruid of the Ancient Order of Druids in America

As far as technological sophistication goes, we consumers of the twenty-first century have it pretty good. We can keep in touch with events on the other side of the world, have great sanitation and medicine, and have millions of books at our fingertips all the time. The downside is that we have very little in the way of true downtime. We have figured out a way to eliminate boredom, but that is not necessarily a good thing. We never have a chance to experience the deserted, forlorn states that lead to greatness. We are too busy to be inspired.

This morning, consider turning off your cell phone, perhaps just for a few minutes or (gasp!) for an hour. Think for a minute about how these devices did not exist a few decades ago, and now we check them every few minutes as though our lives depended on it. See if you can cut back on texting and social media, if only for today. See if a space opens that can be used to ponder something genuinely new.

Walk Down the Path

The surrender of the ego is the most difficult thing we have to do. . . .
The surrender of the ego is the ONLY way of life.

Bede Griffiths, *Hindu-Christian Mystic*

Those of us who feel drawn to the spiritual life have a long and uncertain road ahead. We have no guarantee of success or even of progress. The path goes through dark and lonely places. We face terrible demons that we would rather ignore. The usual comforts of life can be torturous for us. The only consolation is knowing that we are making the journey of the ages, undertaking the process of transformation that is the destiny of every soul.

Today, you have a choice as to whether you will do the work of contemplation or let the time slip by. There are no punishments or rewards other than the natural outcomes of your choices. You only have to ask yourself what you truly want in life and act accordingly. Know that the struggle itself will ennoble your soul, and that, as you struggle to enrich your life, you allow others to do the same.

Offer an Unguarded Heart

Consider our difficulties in the context of the unimaginable scale of the Creation. There is the Milky Way with its 300,000 million stars. . . . Consider, too, the wonder of nature: the 228 separate and distinct muscles in the head of a caterpillar. This world in which we find ourselves is an unimaginable mystery, to which we can only respond with awe and a sense of worshipful attention.

John Lane, Painter, Writer, Educator

We go most of our lives in a kind of mental fog, a narrowing of the scope of our concerns, until we can see only the most pressing matters, only the small confines of our immediate social circle. The universe around us beckons, but we struggle to see and hear it for the glare and the noise of civilization, and a small slice of civilization at that. We must work very hard to keep our eyes and ears open, to see beyond the glare and hear beyond the noise. Only a very discerning heart and mind can sense what truly matters: Such a gift is well worth seeking.

You may have a very pressing schedule this morning: Perhaps you already feel days or weeks behind. Pause right now to say thanks for the things that are going well in your life. Take a moment to notice the beauty around you, no matter how small and insignificant. Realize that the hopes and dreams of billions of other souls are wrapped up in a common destiny with you. Wish everyone and everything well. Be completely unguarded with your heart, if only for a few moments of quiet contemplation.

Look to Truth

Spirituality makes religion behave.

Michael Eric Dyson, Public Intellectual

In order to move past a place of resistance, a closed door, a blockage, either in our personal lives or in broader social struggles, we have to give everything away. We have to push ourselves to the point where we have nothing else to say and nothing left to do. We have to get to the point where the cup is completely empty. Then, miraculously and without fail, the cup is full again. We have to move beyond our reticence, beyond our timidity, and into a place of boldness where we speak our truth and the truth of the communities to which we belong.

This morning, be mindful of the ways in which you may be creating your own obstacles by refusing to use the resources at your disposal. Before you complain of being powerless, take a few minutes to make a list of your assets, which may be time and money, friends and connections, or natural and civic resources. You can build a life for yourself where priority is placed on a mindful and truthful connection to the world around you. You have more power for transformation than you know.

Look for Your Gifts in Disguise

It is madness to put your trust in common sense.
It is madness to have doubts about it. It is madness to look ahead.
It is madness to live without looking.

Boris Pasternak, Author

They say that the devil is in the details. And we all would like to escape from the details sometimes, from needing to file taxes and mow the lawn, from sending e-mails and receiving them, from dealing with the delicate feelings of others and ourselves. And yet life is lived in the details, and a heightened sense of wonder and a keen sense of observation can make the most tedious hour bearable. So we shake hands with the devil, or dance with him, and hope to be spared from the barbs of despair and boredom.

This morning, look at all of the small tasks that will be yours from sunrise to midnight. Rather than shrink back from them or groan at the thought of such drudgery, just take each one as it comes. Resolve to observe your circumstances as they arise, without adding anything, good or bad, by way of judgment or commentary. See if you can regard each circumstance as a gift in disguise, however annoying it might appear on the surface. Remain open to the gift of the present moment, and let go of pessimistic tendencies.

Pay Your Debt to the Earth

The Earth isn't dying; it's being killed, and those who are killing it have names and addresses. What are YOU doing for the earth tonight?

Earth Liberation Front Communiqué, Quoting Utah Phillips, Singer and Activist

Mindfulness practice cannot be separated from our mutual dwelling place on planet Earth. Mindfulness calls us to use no more than we need, to restrain our sense of greed, to live more lightly on the planet. Mindfulness asks us to make amends for past wrongs and to change our way of life. Mindfulness leads back to the planet that gives all things birth, the mother of us all. It also recognizes that we cannot change everything all at once, but this in no way excuses laziness or inaction. We all begin here in this present moment, but we cannot afford to wait any longer to protect our home for future generations.

For a few minutes this morning, meditate on your debt to the Earth's systems. The Earth gives you clean water to drink, safe food to eat, a roof over your head, and, indeed, everything that you have. Resolve this day to repay a small portion of that debt by protecting the Earth, your home. Set the intention in your heart that an opportunity will come your way to act on behalf of the rivers, soil, and animals. When the opportunity comes, act without delay, knowing that you are protecting the source of life itself.

Getting Beyond Surface Spirituality

*As we come to see more clearly our interconnectedness with others,
we develop a greater sense of gratitude for what has been given to us,
a profound sense of sorrow regarding the illusions we collectively live
by, and a greater willingness to change our ways of being in the world
to remove the causes of suffering for ourselves and for our fellow
travelers on this beautiful and fragile planet.*

John Eric Baugher, Sociologist

One of the challenges that has beset the teaching of meditation, especially in the West, has been the tendency to try to extract the *goodies* from meditation—the increased concentration, the stress reduction, etc.—without the cultural "trappings" and the ethics of the dharmic teachings of India. We tend to want the magic without the transformation, the powers without the purpose of these ancient traditions. We want the Buddha in a box, the Om to go, the quick fix. It is my sincere hope that this is only the first phase in what will become a broader transformation of consumer culture, that corporate forays into spirituality will turn into a revaluation of the profit motive and a more holistic model of business.

As you move deeper into your mindfulness practice, you may feel like you are at odds with your home and work life. You will encounter resistance as you implement the insights that have come to you in your practice. Gently work with those places of resistance, making small changes wherever possible. Strive to bring the peace that you have gained into greater realization in the world. Today, you may find yourself moving into a position of leadership as others look to you as a source of peace and stability in your world. It will be up to you to maintain a level head in the midst of adverse circumstances, to be a voice of calm in a frenetic world.

Duty Can Be a Spiritual Calling

There is a shadow side to almost every positive thing we can do for ourselves, including spiritual practice. All spiritual and psychological tools can be used in a "willful" way. . . . [S]ometimes, under the guise of self-care, we are really just checking out: denying what's happening and how scary it feels to show up for life.

Ingrid Mathieu, Psychotherapist

Sometimes life will throw at you the opposite of what you want or think you want. You crave solitude and rest, but you find yourself among people, conducting important business. You want to be an introvert, but your life pushes you to be an extrovert. You would like nothing more than to sit beneath a tree and meditate, but you have to be in a conference room instead. Duty calls, and you cannot walk away from it, at least not yet. So you develop a spirituality of business, a spirituality of relationships, a spirituality of finding the divine where you are instead of where you would like to be.

This morning, you might be feeling like you are not *spiritual* enough. You may feel like your efforts at mindfulness and meditation are insignificant. Sometimes, the best thing you can possibly do is just go to work and take care of the kids. Spirituality doesn't always feel blissful: It can sometimes just be taking care of what needs to be done. Regardless of where you find yourself, your life is being renewed, day by day, into your image of the divine.

Contemplating Global Changes

The cultural transformation from the love of power
to the power of love *is the drama of our time.*

Anodea Judith, Psychologist, Spiritual Teacher

Our planet is in the midst of huge shifts that we have not even begun to grasp. The civilization that we know today will not exist in two hundred years, or it will exist in a completely different form. As this world cycle comes to a close, there will be massive social, economic, and environmental upheavals, the primeval chaos represented by the floods of the ancient scriptures of the world. As all of this happens, we can choose to be reactive and divisive, or we can choose to lovingly embrace change. If we choose the latter, we may not escape unscathed, but we will have the benefit of an increased sense of community and solidarity.

As you read or listen to the news this morning, you may hear about ecological catastrophes, terrorist attacks, and political instability in many parts of the world. Notice what emotional and intellectual responses arise within you. Without judgment or blame, see if you can name your thoughts as fearful, aggressive, sad, or indifferent. Think about what a loving, compassionate response to world events would be. Allow the thought of love and compassion to address you personally, to call you to action.

Listen to Your Inner Guide

We are losing the distinction between urgent and important—now everything gets heaped on the urgent pile. And it's quite frankly easier to do the trivial things that are "urgent" than it is to do the important things. . . . This busywork pulls our attention from the meaningful work—taking time to think, reflect, and imagine.

James Victore, Designer, Filmmaker, Educator

Being unselfish does not mean automatically saying *yes* to any request made of you or dropping all boundaries on your time and energy. It means living according to the best impulses that you have in you. It means using your limited instrument of mind for the greater good, to the best that you are able at this time and place. Sometimes that means making difficult judgment calls about what deserves your time and attention. Sometimes it means sacrificing the good for the great. When making these decisions, keep in mind that your creative work may be the best means that you have to serve humanity.

As you further develop your mindfulness, you may notice a subtle guide arising within your mind and heart, a voice or intuition that feels different from the grumbling voice of the ego. This is the *antaryāmin*, the Inner Guide that is steering you down the right path. This morning, you may feel this guide nudging you in a certain direction: Follow it readily. If you do not feel this guide, ask for it to be made known to you. Maintaining inner silence and constant seeking are conducive to its appearance.

Love Yourself

Mercy to animals means mercy to [hu]mankind.

Henry Bergh, Founder of the American Society for the Prevention of Cruelty to Animals

Mindfulness practice does boost performance and increase creativity, but this only scratches the surface of the transformation that can take place when we practice diligently. We learn eventually to be more kind and understanding with ourselves, which leads to concern for others, and, ultimately, for all creatures who share the Earth with us. When this culture of care reaches critical mass, it will mean no less than transformation of the planet. Humankind will no longer be governed by greed but by concern for human and nonhuman others.

You may notice in yourself this morning a tendency to punish yourself for your problems, perhaps by eating a poor diet or not getting exercise. Perhaps you overwork or underwork. Or maybe you have more serious issues of self-harm. Even if it is difficult to do, cultivate a pure love for yourself, for the entire package of your physical and psychological make-up. Strive to make peace with yourself, and then extend that acceptance to your entire life. Stop the cycle of harming self and others and endeavor to live nonviolently in thought, word, and deed.

Open Spaces, Open Minds

Green-time [time spent outdoors] promotes long-term gains in attention and impulse control—domains which largely shape how well our brain functions, and therefore how well we function in school, work, relationships, and health. Green-time is a truly solid investment in mental wealth.

Victoria L. Dunckley, Psychiatrist

In order for peace to be possible, ambition and greed must be eliminated, or at least greatly restrained. A peaceful frame of mind most easily arises when we can afford a certain leisurely pace, when we can have time to reflect and absorb the beauties of nature. Business beige cubical life must give way, at least some of the time, to lying in the grass and blowing dandelion seeds. This requires individual change, and it requires societal change. Mindfulness is a great prize worth fighting for. How odd is it that we should have to fight for what is most normal and natural? And yet that is the situation in which we find ourselves.

This morning, see if you can get outside for at least half an hour. Lie in a hammock or go for a walk. Sit and read a book or write in your journal while sitting outside. If someone gives you flack for your choice, do not let them get under your skin. You can be effective while taking care of yourself. In the long run, you will be more helpful to others if you maintain your physical and mental health.

Green-time

[time spent outdoors]
promotes long-term gains
in attention and impulse control—
domains which largely shape how well
our brain functions, and therefore how
well we function in school,
work, relationships, and health.
Green-time is a truly solid
investment in mental wealth.

—VICTORIA L. DUNCKLEY,
PSYCHIATRIST

Accept Risk

Shamanic healers insist on the existence of an intelligent Other somewhere in a dimension nearby. The existence of an ecology of souls or a disincarnate intelligence is not something that science can be expected to grapple with and emerge with its own premises intact. Particularly if this Other has long been a part of the terrestrial ecology, present but unseen, a global secret sharer.

Terence McKenna, Ethnobotanist

We can use a rigid epistemology, a conventional way of knowing, as a defense against what we do not understand. If we admit into our consciousness only what can be proven by peer-reviewed, double blind research, we would find that we had excluded much of what makes life worth living. Acceptance of a certain amount of risk attends spiritual exploration: We have to accept that we will have unconventional ideas and procedures, that we may go down dead ends, that we will venture close to the margins of society. We may do things that even those closest to us will find strange. The medicine lies in weirdness.

This morning, you may find yourself at a certain juncture where you feel that you are no longer making progress in the expansion of awareness. At a certain point, you must change your habits or stop growing. You must be willing to live in a different way, to accept a little more risk, to move into the unknown. Ask yourself what you have been unwilling to do up until now. What is it that has the potential to open new avenues of exploration for you? Would you be willing to take a few steps in that direction today?

Welcome Slow, Subtle Shifts

Cultivating the good means recovering the incandescent power of love that is present as a potential in all of us. An awakened life demands a fundamental re-visioning of the limited views we hold of our own potential.

Sharon Salzberg, Buddhist Teacher, Cofounder of Insight Meditation Society

Mindfulness meditation has been accepted by corporate America more than any other branch of living wisdom, but that shouldn't be taken to mean that mindfulness will turn us all into slavish drones. Mindfulness meditation is the first wave of a larger transformation, a foot in the door, so to speak, for those who care about people, the Earth, and animals. The fact that major corporations would employ meditation at all signals a change in awareness beginning to take place. This change is frustratingly slow, but inexorable, as people awaken from the bad dream of greed and destruction and awaken to the possibility of greater respect for each other and for nonhuman life.

At this point in your practice, you have begun to experience sparks of inspiration, little jolts of insight as you shift to living mindfully. You may feel a subtle nudge to change your pattern of living. This morning, think about how you can follow this subtle guidance; it will take courage, but the rewards are great for those who listen to the deepest wisdom of their souls. Listening to the Inner Guide may not make you rich, famous, or powerful, but it will lead you to a place of beauty and peace that is always available to you.

You Have Everything You Need

The world offers perennial renewal, in the grass that pushes itself up between the cracks in the sidewalk, in the end of every torrential rainstorm and in every newly planted window box, in every unexpected revolution, with each new morning's light. This unstoppable spirit of renewal is in you. Trust it.

Jack Kornfield, Buddhist Teacher, Cofounder of Spirit Rock Meditation Center

Meditation or mindfulness really amounts to trust: Trust that the present moment will be enough to satisfy our needs for love and basic provision. The anxious mind withdraws from the present moment and into a fantasy about the future or reconstructions of the past. When we give ourselves to mindfulness, we are saying that we believe that reality can be trusted with our full attention, that we do not need to worry, that we will find life to be hospitable. This basic trust is contagious, and, as we relax into the present, we allow others to do so as well.

This morning, trust that you have everything you need right at your disposal. You are loved, you have enough, and you are enough. Whatever bad things may have happened in the past are not here now. The future does not exist. You only have this moment: Awaken to it, live in it. Trust that you have now and will have everything that you need.

Trust in the Universe to Provide

The Self is not the individual body or mind, but rather that aspect deep inside each person that knows the Truth.

Swami Vishnu-devananda, Founder of Sivananda Yoga Centers

The limited mind believes in the fiction of scarcity: There is a short supply of good ideas, of material goods, of care and love. Belief in this fiction of scarcity causes insecurity, grasping, and hoarding, and so creates what it seeks to avoid. We can let go of the fiction of scarcity and live according to the higher mind, which teaches us that we have an infinite supply to satisfy our needs. We have more than enough good ideas, more than enough food and clothing, more than enough love and attention. All is well if we can only see, and if we can see, we can help others to see as well.

Your limited mind may be giving you trouble this morning, giving you messages of anxiety and insecurity. Release this smaller mind and open yourself to the Mind at the heart of the universe. Know that your guide and protector always lies close at hand, waiting to give you shelter and strength. Whenever you need help this day, allow yourself a few minutes of silent listening. Boldly speak your need into the universe, and you will find a supply waiting for you.

Changing the Camera Angle

Salutations [to the one] who is great and controls the world from behind the veil, who gives us wisdom to cross the sea of domestic life, who knows everything, who carries [all] and who maintains and destroys nature.

Adhi Narayana Sthuthi

Most languages have three persons—first, second, and third (I/we, you, and he/she/it/they). These groupings shift our thinking into believing that these distinctions actually obtain metaphysics. Even if we are not willing to let go of these groupings, we can place them mentally under suspension. We can think, for a little while, that there is no differentiation between the perspectives implied by this terminology. We can think of the simultaneous merging of these three perspectives, and that is what is entailed in mindfulness or meditation.

This morning, picture the room in which you are currently seated from various different perspectives: from *inside* your own body, from overhead, from across the room, etc. See how *all* of these perspectives emanate from *your* mind, which itself emerges from nature. For the rest of the day, try to view yourself as if from the third person, as though you were describing things from a detached perspective. You may not be able to maintain this for very long due to force of habit, but see how long you can see yourself as if from the outside.

Think Like a Tree

*When I dare to be powerful, to use my strength in the service of my vision,
it makes no sense whether or not I am afraid.*

Audre Lorde, Feminist

People can learn a lot from trees. Do not think that they are inert things: Look how their roots grow down into the Earth, providing so much strength. They feel their way through the Earth, finding veins of nutrients and hidden sources of water. Their branches reach upward so stealthily past any obstruction, toward the light. Their leaves respire, exchanging waste for vital breath. See the bark so strong and protective, the branches so beneficent to living things. See how they endure through the years while no one notices. See how they commune with each other through pollen, how they rear their young to be like themselves.

This morning, as you rise to meet your day, look at your habits of thought, word, and deed. See if your actions are in service of your mission in life or whether they depart from your core purpose. Can you identify anything extraneous, anything self-defeating, anything out of harmony? Resolve this day to do only those things that will increase your potential for life and wholeness, just like the tree does. Resolve to do nothing that will harm yourself or others. Live into your full potential as a human being, striving for the highest degree of excellence of which you are capable.

The Branching Lines of Choice

It's not what you look at that matters, it's what you see.

Henry David Thoreau, Transcendentalist

This present moment branches along so many fractal lines: This day and hour hold great potential, the power of a thousand suns. The spiral arms of our choices continue into future generations: They affect all of the orders of nature. Explosive growth radiates from this moment, and only we can decide what the future will look like. We, of course, have our past karmas, but the flip side of past karmas is the infinite variety and possibility of the emerging future. We should not let this great promise become paralyzing but should, instead, throw ourselves into our best tendencies and our most exalted visions.

This morning, you may not feel particularly excited to start the day. You may be feeling dull and tired. You may not feel like you have what it takes to tackle all that you need to do. Picture energy coiled at the base of your spine like a great reserve waiting to be tapped. Feel it pulsating, an orb of brilliant light. As you move the orb up the spine, feel yourself renewed and energized as the fractal lines of your choices extend outward. Think of your energy and enthusiasm for life flowing through you rather than from you. You are a conduit for this energy, not its source.

Shedding Thought

The whole moon and the entire sky
Are reflected in one dewdrop on the grass.

Dogen, Zen Master

What keeps you up at night, worrying, tossing, and turning? What is it that keeps you up at night, exulting, rising to watch and wait? Stop thinking about the thing that makes you worry: Eventually, worry will die. Keep doing the thing that makes your heart sing, and eventually it will become your life. You don't need any support; you don't need more of this and that: You already know the way. Follow your inborn guide, and you will be completely free.

When was the last time you felt so happy that you were dancing for joy? Was it the birth of a child? Visiting your favorite place? What could help you recapture that feeling today? What could put your heart in that place of joy and celebration? See if you can take some small steps today toward recapturing that joy. It's okay if you don't feel like you can get to that joyous place: Do something that will take you a little bit of the way there.

Build Your Concentration Skills

Divine consciousness makes us feel that God is right here, inside each life-breath, inside each heartbeat, inside everyone and everything around us.

Sri Chinmoy, Spiritual Teacher

We have lost the ability to pay attention with the diligence necessary to see the hidden, divine side of things. Painters, poets, and mystics catch glimpses of it. To see properly, we have to discipline the mind, to pick something from nature or culture and concentrate on it exclusively. The object of concentration could be anything—a few lines of scripture, a poem, a rock, a bird, a flower—but the intensity and fervor of concentration make the insight come. Our world, at every turn, will oppose and thwart the total concentration of mind and heart. So the quest for mindfulness will be at odds with the world if it is undertaken seriously.

When a place or an object of human manufacture particularly strikes you, in a way that makes you feel that perhaps the world still holds some beauty and truth, flag that place or object as a possible focus for meditation. Even this morning, you can visit your favorite place or find a few verses to concentrate your mind. Familiarize yourself entirely with the object of meditation so that you can see it even with your eyes closed. Then listen deeply, with complete absorption, waiting for its secret to be revealed. If you are on a tight schedule, set a timer for, say, twenty minutes, and use that time for concentration on the object.

Forget about Whether or Not It's Working

There is a saying, "To catch two birds with one stone." That is what people usually try to do. Because they want to catch too many birds they find it difficult to be concentrated on one activity, and they may end up not catching any birds at all!

Shunryu Suzuki, Sōtō Zen Monk

We can get into an anxious state of mind where we want to know if we will fulfill our goals in life. In spirituality, this is manifested as a desire to know whether or not the practice is *working*, and so we examine ourselves for signs of some sort of enlightenment. This could be true whether we are saying mantras, chanting verses, or sitting for zazen or dhyana. The trouble is that stepping back from the practice actually makes it more difficult to engage with the practice. The hard thing is to just do the practice and not worry about whether or not it is working, and to be fully immersed in life.

Try not to compare yourself with the yardstick of spiritual experiences you may have had in the past, perhaps when you first began your favorite practice. You are not the same person that you were ten or twenty years ago. It's not that those experiences don't matter: It's just that they happened to someone else a long time ago. Try to focus on the realization that you might have today, in this moment. Make today a new occasion for expanding your capacities and increasing your awareness.

Meet Your Subtle Body

So I say: Mind, don't you sleep / Or Time is going to get in and steal from you.

Ramprasad Sen, Hindu Poet

The subtle body, which you might imagine as the energetic shadow of your physical body, can be difficult to perceive because we are so used to thinking about the gross (material) body. We can catch glimpses of the subtle body in meditation. We begin with silence and persist until the blood rushing is heard in the ears. The heartbeat may also be felt and even heard. Dancing lights may be seen in the head region, or whirling colors along the spinal axis. I am not talking about *visualization* (not that there is anything wrong with these techniques) but about simple, direct observation. The body can be seen to exhibit continuous whirling movement within.

You may wonder how to experience the subtle body. The ability to perceive it shows powers of concentration, but it also opens our minds to the deeper reality of the body, that it is not an inert, mechanical thing like a puppet made of wood blocks. We can be so cerebrally focused in our daily lives that we forget that we are not just talking heads atop stick figure bodies. This morning, as you go about your day, pay close attention to the body, especially its more subtle layers, and see if this does not change your thought processes.

Celebrate All Insights and Victories

We can only see a short distance ahead,
but we can see plenty there that needs to be done.

Alan Turing, Computer Scientist

In the coming decades, we will see the merging of humans with computers as never before. We will also see the convergence of many disciplines, so we will approach problems from many angles at once. Meditative states that once took decades to reach will become more accessible as the neurology is understood more readily. This will come with amazing potential, but it will also have new quandaries as more and more people begin to meditate with very rapid success.

Your journey to mindfulness has probably been bumpy at times, but the progress you've made thus far has made you stronger. You have gained some measure of freedom from the reactive emotional states. You have come to know yourself better and have seen through the obstacles in your life. Take a minute to give thanks for the insights and victories that you have had so far, and send good thoughts and prayers to your fellow travelers along the journey to liberation. Send good thoughts that new technologies will become vehicles for heightened spiritual awareness rather than just venues for entertainment and distraction.

Wear the Rich Garment of the Present

What war is this of Thee and Me? Give o'er the wanton strife,
You are the heart within my heart, the life within my life.

Sarojini Naidu, Indian Independence Activist, Poet

The mindfulness practitioner continually fights against inertia, the desire to relax back into distraction and fantasy. Ever vigilant, the mindful sage stays close to the immediate sensorium and to the observation of thought. This work of the instant becomes the work of a lifetime, as the mind must be retrained to stop wandering and stay with the ever-flowing present. The rewards for this practice are great: increased feelings of peace, greater appreciation of beauty, and a deep sense of meaning. Many go down this road, but very few see it to its conclusion.

This morning, as you begin your day, call yourself back to the breath. Call yourself back to whatever you observe right now, either internally or externally. Put distraction away today and live in the moment. Bring your full powers to bear on everything you do. Imagine that you wear the present moment like a rich and colorful garment, and crown yourself with the energy rising through your spinal column. You will be awake and more than awake, alive in the deepest part of your being.

Revising Our Concepts of God

*What if you don't believe that you love yourself? Doesn't matter.
Your role is to lay down the pathways, brick upon brick, reinforce the
connections between the neurons. The mind already has a strong wiring
for love. The body knows it as well. It knows that love nurtures, that love
is gentle, that love is accepting. It knows that love heals.*

Kamal Ravikant, Entrepreneur, Angel Investor

Many of us in the West grew up with a conflicted image of God, in which we were told simultaneously that God was loving and forgiving, but also vengeful and jealous. We were told that we were inherently sinful and would never quite be good enough. We were told that violence could be salvific and that some people were just not chosen and hence could be dismissed. Little wonder, then, that many of us struggle to reconcile this fractured picture of the divine. Mindfulness practice helps us observe our inherited images of God and see what effects these paradigms of divinity might be having on our lives.

Think about your earliest memories of religion, when someone first told you about God or some idea of the transcendent. Do you still hold the same idea about ultimate reality, or has it changed over the years? Is your image of the divine serving you or harming you? Now that you are an adult, you are free to have beliefs (or lack thereof) that make you feel supported and loved. For a few minutes this morning, think about what it would feel like to be completely surrounded with love and affection. Give yourself the freedom to craft an image of divinity that matches with this feeling.

What if you don't
believe that you love yourself?
Doesn't matter.
Your role is to lay down the pathways,
brick upon brick, reinforce the
connections between the neurons.
The mind already has a strong wiring for love.
The body knows it as well.
It knows that love nurtures,
that love is gentle, that love is accepting.
It knows that *love heals*.

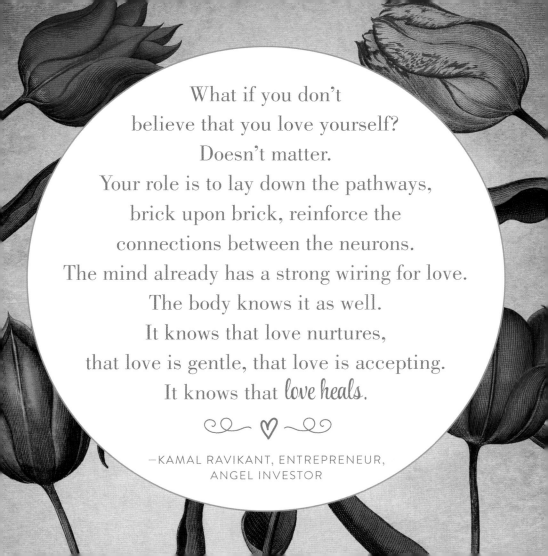

—KAMAL RAVIKANT, ENTREPRENEUR,
ANGEL INVESTOR

Reflect on Your Ups and Downs

Faith is the opposite of resentment, cynicism, and negativity. Faith is always, finally, a self-fulfilling prophecy. Faith actually begins to create what it desires. Faith always recreates the good world. Without faith, you sink into the bad world that you most feared.

Richard Rohr, Franciscan Priest, Founder of the Center for Action and Contemplation

A lot of crushingly bad things happen in the world: people get cancer (even kids), people kill each other (for spare change), and people destroy the Earth (the one and only). To choose faith over despair is not to put on rose-colored glasses. People of faith (whether that faith is religious or not—atheists, too, have faith in certain ideals) choose to believe because unbelief is just too painful to bear. We all need reasons to get out of bed in the morning, and, for that reason, we all must believe in some kind of ideal. Magical things happen when some wild-eyed fantasy takes flight because some dreamer kept at a harebrained scheme long enough and hard enough to make it happen.

As you look back on your life, you undoubtedly see periods of light and dark, periods of intense inspiration followed by depths of despair. For some people, the troughs and peaks may be higher or lower, but everyone has them. What keeps you going through the dark times? What gets you up in the morning? Take a few minutes to reflect on your personal life's wisdom. That spark of inspiration that has saved you, time and again, may be the message that you have to share with the world.

The Dark Parts of Your Life Can Offer Blessings

All thoughts, all passions, all delights, / Whatever stirs this mortal frame, / All are but ministers of Love, / And feed his sacred flame.

Samuel Taylor Coleridge, Poet, Philosopher

Spiritually-inclined people get into all sorts of bargaining with God (or the gods, or the Universe, or Higher Power, or the Buddha, or life, or alter egos, etc.), saying, "I don't want all of this despair: Send me the good stuff. Send me happiness and joy and bliss." And, with the growth of the prosperity movement, this bargaining might look like, *I don't want to manage my money: Make me fabulously wealthy instead.* Or maybe it is some sort of contract: *God, if you do x for me, I swear I'll do y for you.* All of this behavior is extremely common, it is not limited to religious people, and it is rooted in self-will and a refusal to surrender to reality.

The sane and sober way to live, which is often not very much fun, is to look at reality first and then make plans around that. Look at your own life. What have you been avoiding? What are the ugly and depressing parts of your life? Those might be the exact places where God (or insert your pre-ferred term here) is trying to meet you. When you accept your situation as it is and do not flee from it, you can meet problems in concrete, constructive ways. This is the mindfulness that hurts, that is difficult, and yet it gives the biggest blessing.

Using Mindfulness to Address Addiction

The soul ripens in tears.

H.P. Blavatsky, Theosophist

If you come from a family struggling with some sort of addiction, whether it is addiction to alcohol, drugs, food, gambling, or any other compulsive behavior, chances are that maladaptive behavior has made its way down to you. There is also a good chance that it has changed forms, making it harder to spot. Mindfulness can be useful in recognizing the ways in which we cling to compulsive behavior to avoid the root of the problem, in letting go of the psychic armor that addiction provides. Mindfulness does not mean analyzing the problem *ad nauseam* (although analysis certainly has its place). It just means saying, "Oh, I'm doing it again," and then gently redirecting the wayward mind toward a less destructive behavior or thought process.

Perhaps you have already recognized that you have some addictive behaviors (most people do). Be gentle with yourself, recognizing that self-blame and guilt actually reinforce the behavior. Get professional help if you need to. This morning, allow grace to flood into your life. You can do this by directing love and forgiveness toward yourself and toward all of those who you feel have wronged you. Breathe deeply into those places of hurt and anger, and open yourself to the genuine possibility of change.

Being Mindful of Addictive Tendencies

Creative work, which many describe as addictive, often swings between grandiosity and disgust with what one does (or who one is) and substance abuse provides outlets and openings. Meditation, like creativity, is addictive and liberating and those who practice discover benefits and pitfalls.

Michael Eigen, Psychotherapist

A euphoric high can be gained from meditation, without any sort of pharmacological intervention. This is true even of mindfulness practice, considered by some to be a benign form of spiritual practice. Practicing meditation requires discernment so that the practitioner can know whether he or she is taking a flight into meditation to avoid doing some *ordinary* work in the world. Spiritual seekers should try to integrate the practice fully into worldly concerns and relationships so that mindfulness becomes a matrix uniting the disparate parts of life rather than a wedge driving them apart. People with addictive tendencies should beware of the tendency to use meditation in the same way as a narcotic drug.

Ask yourself whether your spiritual practice is integrated into your life. Does it increase your capacity for love and relationships, or does it detract? Does it make you more productive and engaged at work, or does it pull you away? Are you able to care for yourself and still engage in the practice? You should return to these open questions at periodic intervals as you seek to move deeper into your mindfulness practice. Over time, you should be able to be immersed in the world while holding on to mindfulness.

Finding Inspiration in Dull and Dreary Times

People think I'm disciplined. It is not discipline.
It is devotion. There is a great difference.

Luciano Pavarotti, Operatic Tenor

When life becomes mere repetition, when it becomes dreary and dull, stay with that feeling. In creative pursuits, in relationships, in work, oftentimes we reach a place where it feels like the well has run dry, as if we have nothing left to give. If we do not let go, something good begins to happen. The needed inspiration appears out of nowhere. A solution to the problem arises. Suddenly what seemed so lifeless now has a purpose. In this struggle with emptiness, growth happens at the last hour, when all seemed lost.

This morning, you may be aware of some dull and dry places in your life. Perhaps some voices in your head are already telling you to give up. Press into that place of boredom and restlessness: See if you can observe it more clearly and bring its contours into focus. Perhaps you can find some words or an image to describe it. Once you have it clearly in view, remain there with that feeling. Breathe into it, accept it. Welcome it. After you have sat with that feeling for a little while, just go about your day. You may find some unexpected way of dealing with the problem.

Live Your Life Without an Escape Hatch

If a man [sic] is at heart just, then in so far is he God; the safety of God, the immortality of God, the majesty of God do enter into that man with justice. If a man dissemble, deceive, he deceives himself, and goes out of acquaintance with his own being. . . . The man who renounces himself, comes to himself.

Ralph Waldo Emerson, Essayist, Poet

We spend too much of our lives trying to find the easy way out, the shortcut to happiness. If we would just put that energy into paying attention, into dealing with present realities, we could transcend troubles much more easily. By seeking to find easy solutions to the problems of life, we cut ourselves off from the main flow of the spirit, which works through difficulty and not in spite of it. Heaven favors the person who does not shrink from pain and disquiet, but who endures patiently, slowly transforming the world through inner refinement. *Heaven* is not some separate eternal realm, but the harmony of the inner and outer life and the discipline of acceptance and contentment.

Perhaps you find yourself seeking an *escape hatch* from the problems of life. You might have some great physical or emotional pain, an intractable problem that endures despite your best efforts. Mindfulness practice teaches you to look directly at that pain, to observe and understand it completely. Take a hard look at your pain and sadness this morning. After you have looked at it for some time, it will still be there, but its sting will be lessened. By observing pain, you cease to identify with it.

Be Kind to Your Mind

My own heart let me have more pity on; let / Me live to my sad self hereafter kind, / Charitable; not live this tormented mind / With this tormented mind tormenting yet. / . . . Soul, self . . . I do advise / You, jaded, let be; call off thoughts awhile / Elsewhere; leave comfort root-room. . . .

Gerard Manley Hopkins, Poet, Jesuit Priest

We have to learn to be gentle with our own minds. Our minds have amazing capabilities, but they are, in the final analysis, fragile instruments that can be damaged when overloaded. So we have to avoid overworking them by trying to do too many things at one time. We have to reduce the necessary *bandwith* so the processing will all go smoothly. We can do this by focusing on one object, by reducing the reactive emotions, and by working diligently and patiently. We also must realize that our limited minds are partial aspects of the mind of nature, and we must draw on this larger mind for strength and inspiration.

Notice the ways that you might damage or punish your mind, by making it do too much, by leaving things until the last minute, by whipping your emotions into a frenzy, or by some other crazy-making behavior. Resolve to be kinder to your own mind, avoiding any behavior that induces anxiety and stress. Change your patterns of thinking and working so that you have maximal ease within the context of the duties assigned to you. When you are in the midst of intense work, take breaks for meditation and physical exercise. Be kind to your mind, and it will be kind to you.

Starting Over Again

You are your own friend and your own enemy.
You must work, but remain as if you had done no work.

Yogaswami of Sri Lanka, Hindu Saint

When some small shade of guilt arises in your mind and heart, it will do no good to hold onto it: Guilt produces no positive results. The feeling will go away by itself with mindfulness practice. Simply observe the feeling and any thoughts associated with it. Pursue positive actions in your life, and guilt will have no hold over you. Over time, you will come to concentrate on having good thoughts and feelings rather than dwelling on the past.

Give thanks this morning for the opportunity to begin again. Know that the past is gone and exists in the mind alone. Give yourself the permission to start over, as though you were just born. Today you can be a new person, no longer beholden to old thoughts and feelings, no longer trapped in the same patterns of action. Resolve to live into your higher nature, as a person filled with divine truth.

Look Beyond Carrot and Stick

Lead, kindly Light, amid the encircling gloom, / Lead Thou me on! / The night is dark, and I am far from home— / Lead Thou me on. / Keep Thou my feet; I do not ask to see / The distant scene—one step enough for me.

J.H. Newman, Roman Catholic Cardinal

We cause our own troubles by looking upon some people as deserving and others as undeserving. Similarly, we paint some situations with shades of dread and anxiety, and others we view as pleasant and satisfying. We bifurcate the world into *good* and *bad*. We seek the carrot and avoid the stick. But this strategy leads to discontent most of the time: The carrot is always distant, and the stick still hurts. Instead, we should seek to be nowhere else than where we are at the time, and to reduce our need for incentives and disincentives. If we remain tied to the present moment, we will find a hidden source of consolation there.

This morning, you may find your mind wandering ahead to coming home in the evening or to the vacation you plan to take in the summertime. Gently bring it back again, to this place and time. Notice the small joys around you. Take the bird in the hand rather than chasing after the one in the bush. Don't go after the next shiny object that appears to distract you from your purpose. Hold to mindful attention no matter what happens.

For more information and further reading, see
http://anahatachakrasatsanga.org/bibliography/

•